Thomas Archer

Pictures and Royal Portraits Illustrative of English and Scottish History

From the Introduction of Christianity to the Present Time: Volume II.

Thomas Archer

Pictures and Royal Portraits Illustrative of English and Scottish History
From the Introduction of Christianity to the Present Time; Volume II.

ISBN/EAN: 9783337020842

Printed in Europe, USA, Canada, Australia, Japan

Cover: Foto ©ninafisch / pixelio.de

More available books at **www.hansebooks.com**

PICTURES
AND
ROYAL PORTRAITS

ILLUSTRATIVE OF

ENGLISH AND SCOTTISH HISTORY,

FROM THE INTRODUCTION OF CHRISTIANITY TO THE PRESENT TIME.

ENGRAVED
FROM IMPORTANT WORKS BY DISTINGUISHED MODERN PAINTERS, AND FROM
AUTHENTIC STATE PORTRAITS.

WITH DESCRIPTIVE HISTORICAL SKETCHES,

BY

THOMAS ARCHER,
AUTHOR OF APPENDIX TO DE BONNECHOSE'S "HISTORY OF FRANCE," ETC

VOLUME II.

LONDON:
BLACKIE & SON: OLD BAILEY;
GLASGOW AND EDINBURGH.
1880.

LIST OF THE PLATES,

WITH

NOTES ON THE ORIGINAL PICTURES AFTER WHICH THEY ARE ENGRAVED.

VOLUME SECOND.

	PAGE
PORTRAIT OF CHARLES II., ... *Frontispiece*,	1

    This engraving is from a drawing made by J. L. Williams in the year 1871, from contemporary prints by Becket and Loggan, after the portrait by Sir Godfrey Kneller. The background is from stamped Spanish leather of the seventeenth century, the border from the frame of a looking-glass in Windsor Castle that belonged to Charles II.

LORD WILLIAM RUSSELL RECEIVING THE SACRAMENT PRIOR TO HIS
    EXECUTION, ... 14

    The original picture, painted by Alexander Johnston, was first exhibited at the Royal Academy in the year 1845, and is now in the National Gallery,—Vernon Collection. It is 5 feet 2 inches wide, and 3 feet 7½ inches high.

PORTRAIT OF JAMES II., ... 18

    This engraving is from a drawing made by J. L. Williams in the year 1873, from contemporary prints by Loggan & White, after pictures by Sir Godfrey Kneller and Sir Peter Lely. The background is from stamped leather of Spanish workmanship of the seventeenth century. The border is adapted from carvings by Grinling Gibbons, in Windsor Castle.

THE ARREST OF ALICE LISLE, ... 24

    The original picture is a fresco painted by E. M. Ward, R.A., on the wall of the Commons' Corridor of the Houses of Parliament, in the year 1857. It is 7 feet 7½ inches wide, by 6 feet 7¼ inches high. A finished sketch for the fresco was exhibited at the Royal Academy in the year 1858.

THE RELEASE OF THE SEVEN BISHOPS, ... 30

    The original picture is a fresco painted by E. M. Ward, R.A., on the wall of the Commons' Corridor of the Houses of Parliament, in the year 1867. It is 7 feet 7¼ inches wide, by 6 feet 8 inches high.

PORTRAIT OF WILLIAM III., ... 36

    The original picture, painted by Sir Godfrey Kneller, is in St. George's Hall, Windsor Castle. The background is from stamped leather of Spanish workmanship of the seventeenth century, in South Kensington Museum, the border from carvings by Grinling Gibbons, in Windsor Castle.

LIST OF THE PLATES.

PAGE

PORTRAIT OF QUEEN MARY II., ... 40

    The original picture, painted by Sir Godfrey Kneller, is in St. George's Hall, Windsor Castle. The background is from stamped leather of Spanish workmanship of the seventeenth century, the border from carvings by Grinling Gibbons, in Windsor Castle.

THE LORDS AND COMMONS OFFERING THE CROWN TO WILLIAM AND MARY, ... 44

    The original picture is a fresco painted by E. M. Ward, R.A., on the wall of the Commons' Corridor of the Houses of Parliament, in the year 1866. It is 7 feet 7 inches wide, by 6 feet 8 inches high.

THE BATTLE OF LA HOGUE, ... 48

    The original picture, painted by Benjamin West, P.R.A., about the year 1774, is considered one of his finest works from English History. The original—for he painted several replicas—was executed for Earl Grosvenor, and continues to adorn the fine collection of that nobleman's successor, the Duke of Westminster. The size of the painting is 6 feet 11 inches in width, by 5 feet in height.

PORTRAIT OF QUEEN ANNE, ... 52

    This engraving is from a drawing made by J. L. Williams in the year 1871, from the marble statue by Ryssbrack at Blenheim House, the seat of the Duke of Marlborough. The background is from stamped leather in South Kensington Museum, of a few years earlier date than the reign of Queen Anne. The border is from a frame in the library at Blenheim.

PORTRAIT OF GEORGE I., ... 58

    The original picture, painted by Sir Godfrey Kneller, is in St. George's Hall, Windsor Castle. The background is from stamped leather of Spanish workmanship of the seventeenth century in South Kensington Museum, the border from panelling at Blenheim House.

THE ESCAPE OF LORD NITHSDALE FROM THE TOWER, A.D. 1716, . . 64

    The original picture, painted by Miss E. M. Osborne, was first exhibited at the Royal Academy in 1861. The size of the painting is 4 feet 10 inches in height, by 3 feet 6 inches in width.

PORTRAIT OF GEORGE II., ... 66

    The original picture, painted by Zeeman, is in St. George's Hall, Windsor Castle. The background is from stamped leather of Spanish workmanship of the seventeenth century in South Kensington Museum, the border from panelling at Blenheim House.

DRAWING A LOTTERY IN GUILDHALL, LONDON, A.D. 1739, ... 70

    This engraving is from a drawing made by J. L. Williams, in the year 1871, from a rare contemporary, but anonymous print, preserved in the British Museum.

FIRST MEETING OF PRINCE CHARLES WITH FLORA MACDONALD, . . 76

    The original picture, painted by Alexander Johnston, was first exhibited at the Royal Academy in the year 1846. Its size is 7 feet 6 inches in width, by 5 feet 6 inches in height.

RELICS ASSOCIATED WITH PRINCE CHARLES EDWARD, ... 78

    The original is a drawing made for this work, by J. L. Williams, in the year 1875. The greater number of these relics are drawn from the objects themselves, in various private collections.

LIST OF THE PLATES.   vii

                                                          PAGE
THE DEATH OF GENERAL WOLFE, ...   84

    The original picture was painted by Benjamin West, P.R.A., in 1770, for Earl Grosvenor, and still adorns the fine collections of that nobleman's successor, the Duke of Westminster. It is considered the painter's masterpiece. A replica of this picture was painted for King George III., and is now at Hampton Court. The size of the picture is 7 feet wide, by 4 feet 7½ inches high.

PORTRAIT OF GEORGE III., ... 86

    The original picture, painted by Allan Ramsay, is in the City Library, Guildhall, London. The background is from damask satin of the period, in South Kensington Museum. The border is adapted from frames in Windsor Castle.

WASHINGTON CROSSING THE DELAWARE, ... 90

    The original picture was painted by E. Leutze at Dusseldorf, in 1850. It is now in the collection of Marshall O. Roberts, Esq., New York. Its size is about 20 feet long, by 12 feet high.

THE DEATH OF MAJOR PIERSON AT ST. HELIERS, JERSEY, ... 94

    The original picture was painted by John Singleton Copely, R.A., about the year 1780, and is considered one of his finest works. It is now in the National Gallery. Its size is 11 feet 11 inches wide, by 8 feet 1 inch high.

NELSON BOARDING THE *San Josef* AT THE BATTLE OF ST. VINCENT, . 96

    The original picture, painted by George Jones, R.A., was presented by the British Institution, in 1835, to Greenwich Hospital. It is now in the Naval Gallery at Greenwich. Its size is 7 feet 3 inches wide, by 5 feet 3 inches high.

THE BATTLE OF THE NILE, ... 100

    The original picture, painted by George Arnald, A.R.A., about the year 1822, was presented by the British Institution, in 1827, to Greenwich Hospital. It is now in the Naval Gallery at Greenwich. Its size is 8 feet 7 inches wide, by 6 feet 1 inch high.

SIR DAVID BAIRD DISCOVERING THE BODY OF TIPPOO SULTAUN, . . 104

    The original picture, painted by Sir David Wilkie, R.A., was first exhibited at the Royal Academy in 1839. It is now at Newbyth, Midlothian, one of the residences of the Baird family. Its size is 11 feet 4½ inches high, by 8 feet 9 inches wide.

THE PRESS-GANG, ... 108

    The original picture, painted by Alexander Johnston, was first exhibited at the Royal Academy in the year 1858. It is now in the collection of James Duncan, Esq., Benmore, Argyleshire. Its size is 4 feet 6 inches high, by 3 feet 11 inches wide.

THE DEFENCE OF SARAGOSSA, 1808–9, ... 112

    The original picture, painted by Sir David Wilkie, R.A., was first exhibited at the Royal Academy in 1829. It was purchased by King George IV., and now forms part of the royal collection in Buckingham Palace. It measures 4 feet 7½ inches in width, by 3 feet 1 inch in height.

WATERLOO—THE DECISIVE CHARGE OF THE LIFE-GUARDS, ... 118

    The original picture, painted by Luke Clennell in the year 1816, is considered the finest of all that artist's works. The power with which an idea of motion is conveyed is very remarkable.

b

LIST OF THE PLATES.

	PAGE

PORTRAIT OF GEORGE IV., ... 122

> The original picture, painted by Sir Thomas Lawrence, P.R.A., is in the Waterloo Gallery, Windsor Castle. The background is from damask satin, in South Kensington Museum, the border from the semicircular saloon in Buckingham Palace.

THE BOMBARDMENT OF ALGIERS, BY LORD EXMOUTH, IN 1816, . . . 128

> The original picture, painted by George Chambers about the year 1832, is now in the Naval Gallery, Greenwich Hospital. Its size is 8 feet 2 inches in width, by 5 feet 8 inches in height.

PORTRAIT OF WILLIAM IV., ... 134

> The original picture, painted by Sir David Wilkie, R.A., was first exhibited at the Royal Academy in 1832. It is now in the Waterloo Chamber, Windsor Castle.

PORTRAIT OF QUEEN VICTORIA, ... 142

> The original picture, painted by Winterhalter about the year 1845, is now in the throne-room, Windsor Castle. The background is adapted from decorations in the Waterloo Chamber, the flowers and fruit in the border from carvings by Grinling Gibbons. The devices in the border consist of the stars of the orders of the Garter, Bath, St. Andrew, St. Patrick, St. Michael, St. George, Star of India, and that of St. George belonging to the Garter, also the badges of the Bath, St. Andrew, and St. Patrick.

QUEEN VICTORIA'S FIRST COUNCIL, ... 146

> The original picture, painted by Sir David Wilkie, R.A., by command of Her Majesty, Queen Victoria, was first exhibited at the Royal Academy in 1838. It now forms part of Her Majesty's collection in Windsor Castle. Its size is 7 feet 10½ inches wide, by 5 feet 0¼ inch high.

PORTRAIT OF ALBERT, PRINCE CONSORT, ... 156

> The original picture, painted by Winterhalter about the year 1846, is now in the throne-room, Windsor Castle. The background and border are adapted from decorations in the Waterloo Chamber, Windsor Castle.

SUNDAY IN THE BACKWOODS OF CANADA, ... 162

> The original picture, painted by Thomas Faed, R.A., was first exhibited at the Royal Academy in 1859. Its size is 4 feet 8 inches, by 3 feet 5½ inches.

GRAND DURBAR AT CAWNPORE, 3D NOVEMBER, 1859, ... 168

> The original picture is a drawing in water colours, painted by Marshall Claxton in 1861, for the publishers of this work. Its size is 1 foot 3 inches by 11½ inches.

. The backgrounds and borders of the portraits in this volume are adapted so as to be in keeping with the series of portraits of the Tudor sovereigns in the Prince's Chamber of the New Palace of Westminster, which are reproduced in the first volume of this work.

HISTORICAL PAPERS.

VOLUME SECOND.

	PAGE
The Restoration,	1
The Execution of Lord Russell,	10
James II.,	18
Alice Lisle,	21
The Seven Bishops,	26
England's New Era,	34
The Battle of La Hogue,	46
Queen Anne,	49
George I.,	56
The Escape of Lord Nithsdale from the Tower,	60
George II.,	65
English Public Lotteries,	69
Charles Edward the Young Pretender,	73
The Death of General Wolfe,	80
George III.,	85
Washington crossing the Delaware,	89
Death of Major Pierson,	93
Nelson boarding the *San Josef*,	94
The Battle of the Nile,	97
The Death of Tippoo Sultaun,	102
The "Press-gang,"	107
The Defence of Saragossa,	110
The Battle of Waterloo,—Decisive Charge of the Life-Guards,	113
George IV.,	120
The Bombardment of Algiers,	126
William IV.,	132
Queen Victoria,	141
Prince Albert,	148
Sunday in the Backwoods,	159
The Grand Durbar at Cawnpore,	166

PICTURES

AND

ROYAL PORTRAITS.

THE RESTORATION.

A NEW period of English history may be said to have dated from the restoration of Charles II. to the throne; not that he either represented or encouraged the advancement of liberty, virtue, or constitutional government, but because the principles which supported all three had been already affirmed; and even the reign of a Stuart, who, like the Bourbons, "learned nothing and forgot nothing," was unable to do worse than temporarily to retard the growing desire for freedom and the extension of commercial activity which were the two most striking manifestations of the time.

A sense of present evils, and a strong apprehension of still greater evils close at hand, had produced an alliance between the Cavaliers and the Presbyterians. Some Presbyterians had been disposed to such an alliance even before the death of Charles I., but it was not till after the retirement of Richard Cromwell that the whole party became eager for the restoration of the royal house. It seemed but too likely that England would fall under the most odious and degrading of all kinds of government,—a government uniting the evils of despotism to the evils of anarchy. At the same time there was a decided reaction against the stern and grim oppression of the stricter sectaries, and those interdictions by which the Puritan legislators dealt, not only with serious vices, but with many pleasant social observances which they chose to assume gave opportunities for vice. Because they were virtuous, there should be no more cakes and ale. The May-poles were hewn down, public amusements were mostly prohibited, the use of the Book of Common Prayer was forbidden not only in churches but in private houses, works of art were defaced and destroyed, holidays were no longer to be observed except as the parliament dictated, and Christmas-day was ordered to be kept as a fast instead of as the great national festival, the season of carols, mirth, loving-kindness, and good cheer.

The cry of the whole people was for a free parliament, and there can be no doubt that while the existing government and the army were opposed to the restoration of the House of Stuart, and were almost equally opposed to each other, the nation had begun to perceive that the best way in which it could escape from the assumptions of an irregular legislature, or the threatened military domination of a formidable soldiery, was to demand such a constitution as Cromwell desired to establish, but to which neither a fanatic parliament nor an equally fanatic army would adhere. Had the army been united in its claims it would have been irresistible; but the army of Scotland and the army in London were divided in opinion, and the former was not only less fanatic, but had regarded with indignation the assumption of the soldiers who strove to bear rule because they happened to be near Westminster instead of on the north of the Tweed. They had no sympathy with the series of revolutions with which the country was threatened, and their general, George Monk, was no zealot, since he had served the king, had been made prisoner by the Roundheads, and had then accepted a commission under the parliament. It may be said that he was a slow-blooded time-server, and his enemies doubtless did say so, while his after career proved that they were not far wrong; but at all events his decision at an important crisis of English history probably saved this country from a devastating civil war, which was well escaped even by the restoration of Charles II.

He refused to acknowledge the authority of the usurper, and at the head of 7000 veterans marched into England, a movement which at once served to test the sincerity of the nation and its eager desire to escape from the oppressive domination under which it suffered. Everywhere the people refused to pay taxes, the apprentices of the city assembled by thousands and clamoured for a free parliament, the fleet sailed up the Thames and declared against the tyranny of the soldiers. The soldiers, no longer under the control of one commanding mind, separated into factions. Every regiment, afraid less it should be left alone a mark for the vengeance of the oppressed nation, hastened to make a separate peace. The military power now gave way to the civil power. Monk marched towards London, but had not yet stated his object or his determination. The cry of the whole people was for a free parliament, and when at length he declared himself to be at one with them the whole nation was wild with delight. The bells rang joyously, the gutters ran with ale, and night after night the sky five miles round London was reddened by innumerable bonfires.

Writs were issued for a general election, and the new parliament, which, having been called without the royal writ, is more accurately described as the convention of 1660, met at Westminster. The lords repaired to the hall from which they had for more than eleven years been excluded by force. Both houses instantly invited the king to return to his country. A gallant fleet conveyed him from Holland to the coast of Kent. When he landed, the cliffs of Dover were covered by thousands of gazers, among whom scarcely one could be found who was not weeping with delight. The journey to London was a continued triumph. The whole road from Rochester was bordered by booths and tents, and looked like an interminable fair. Everywhere flags were flying, bells and music sounding, wine and ale flowing in rivers to the health of him whose return was the return of peace, law, and freedom.[1]

It was on the 25th of May that Charles and his two brothers, the Dukes of York and Gloucester, landed near Dover, where Monk met them. The king embraced and kissed his restorer, calling him "Father." On the 29th, which was Charles' birth-day, and that on which he completed his thirtieth year, he made his solemn entry into London, attended by the members of both houses, by bishops, ministers, knights of the Bath, lord-mayor and aldermen, kettle-drums and trumpets.

It would have been well if Charles had sincerely endeavoured to justify the prognostications of happiness which accompanied his restoration; but except that he was too apparently easy and indifferent to usurp an authority which would have led first to persecution and afterwards to another revolution, his conduct was little calculated to maintain or to restore to England the place which she had gained amidst the nations of Europe, or to give the people that sense of security for their liberties which they had hoped to attain. With an

[1] Macaulay.

air of careless good nature and almost languid idleness he contrived by a kind of cynical cunning to play off ministers and parties against each other and to gain his own selfish ends. A slothful debauchee whose court was a scandal, and living in an atmosphere of sensualism and duplicity, he yet contrived to preserve a reputation for kindness. With a face and appearance which suggested anything but cheerfulness, his ready affability and complete courtesy, together with a pleasant way of saying those personally witty things to which modern language has given the name of "chaff," enabled him to hold his own with less difficulty than he would have encountered if anybody had really believed him to be in earnest.

Temple said that "he desired nothing but that he might be easy himself, and that everybody else should be so;" but this is only a superficial estimate of his character. Perhaps it would be more correct to say that he encouraged other people to be easy lest he should otherwise interfere with his own ease. He temporized, made concessions, evaded decided issues, and waited and watched till, by skilfully availing himself of the course of events, he seemed to have been released by them rather than to have released himself from his engagements. Popular suspicion of any designs of his own was effectually disarmed by his seemingly idle habits and his cheerful affability. Who could have suspected a royal conspirator in the chatty man of pleasure feeding the ducks in St. James' Park! Nature had attempted to mark the true character of the man by the grim sardonic features with which she endowed him: but he persuaded his people to disbelieve in the evidence of nature.

But if he deluded his own people, he deluded foreign powers also. He was, it is well known, the pensioner of France; but it is an entire mistake to suppose that he was the mere servile tool of Louis. He was too shrewd to resort to the systematic illegalities of his father to obtain extra parliamentary supplies, and he resolved to achieve his end out of the coffers of Louis. He cared little for the degradation to himself, of such a position in the eyes of France, or of his own people, when it was accidentally disclosed to them. He was resolved not to be wholly dependent on Louis any more than on the House of Commons, and he played off the one resource against the other with marvellous skill and success. Louis, in fact, could scarcely count more surely on Charles' support, as the reward of his money payments, than he could on that of the popular leaders whom he also paid for opposing their king.

The conventional aspect in which most questions presented themselves to the mind of Charles had at least one good effect. They rendered him comparatively unsusceptible to the feelings of resentment and implacability. Naturally good tempered, and in his familiar social intercourse willing to bear defeat in his encounters of wit with good humour, he did not, as a rule, feel any personal grudge to those who thwarted or opposed his political schemes. He was cold-hearted enough, it is true, to pronounce their doom with calm indifference, if policy seemed to render their removal desirable; but apart from this he avoided the shedding of blood, and would seldom condescend to remember personal injuries. The man who had condemned his father to the scaffold he sent to a cruel death with entire phlegm, though in so doing he probably followed a policy of royal self-assertion, and consulted the demands of excited partisans, rather than those of his own feelings. He did not press the sentence on Lambert, while he pronounced the greatest possible panegyric on the abilities and character of Vane, in declaring him to be in his opinion too dangerous a man to let live. Russell and Sidney suffered probably less from any fear of their personal ability than from a strong belief in their influence as the heads of a party which, but for their removal, might have succeeded after the king's death in preventing the succession of the Duke of York. On this latter point Charles had followed his usual policy of balancing pretensions and keeping his real purpose in suspense. He had indulged his own fondness for Monmouth freely, and in so doing had held in check the intrigues of James and the uncompromising party who gathered round that prince; while he never allowed Monmouth to assume the position of his intended heir.[1]

At the same time Charles II. cannot well be regarded as an astute plotter. He was utterly without ambition. He detested business, and such was his apparent ignorance of affairs that the clerks of the council could scarcely forbear sneering at him as he sat playing with one of his pet spaniels or making frivolous remarks while the affairs of the nation demanded attention. He wished to be a king such as Louis XV. afterwards was, a king who could draw without limit on the treasury for the gratification of his private tastes, who

[1] Sanford.

could hire with wealth and honours persons capable of assisting him to kill the time, and who, even when the state was brought by maladministration to the depths of humiliation and to the brink of ruin, could still exclude unwelcome truth from the purlieus of his own seraglio.

Yet he was a slave without being a dupe. Worthless men and women, whom he knew to be destitute of affection for him and undeserving of his confidence, could easily wheedle him out of titles, places, domains, state secrets, and pardons. In the religious disputes which divided his Protestant subjects his conscience was not at all interested. For his opinions oscillated in suspense between infidelity and Popery; and at last he died in the profession of the Romish faith, attended by the priest, who, having once saved his life at Boscobel, was brought clandestinely and in disguise to his death-bed to hear his confession. His character for a kind of satirical wit mingled with a peculiar and exquisite courtesy, was sustained to the last, if we are to believe the generally received statement, that he apologized to his courtiers and gentlemen "for being such an unconscionable time dying." Indeed this perfect courtesy had been the charm which many times had enabled the king to set aside even the public indignation provoked by his actions, and the easy good nature of a disposition which was perhaps indifferent to qualities that it did not itself possess to some extent excused the immoralities of his life.

Charles, who was incapable of love in the highest sense of the word, was the slave of any woman whose person excited his desires, and whose airs and prattle amused his leisure. Indeed a husband would be justly derided who should bear from a wife of exalted rank and spotless virtue half the insolence which the King of England bore from concubines who, while they owed everything to his bounty, caressed his courtiers almost before his face. It would not be profitable to extract from the pages of Grammont passages which show the condition of the court and of society at that time. Many of the pert quaint passages in Pepys' *Diary* are suggestive enough of the riot and debauchery which was too gross to represent the luxury that sometimes makes sin dazzling, and too low for the appearance of refinement by which vice may conceal its deformities. There are few more striking descriptions than those brief entries made by Evelyn in his *Diary* respecting the death-bed at Whitehall; and a page or two further on he remarks, "I can never forget the inexpressible luxury and profaneness, gaming and all dissoluteness, and as it were total forgetfulness of God (it being Sunday evening), which this day se'nnight I was witness of, the king sitting and toying with his concubines, Portsmouth, Cleveland, Mazarine, &c., a French boy singing love songs in that glorious gallery, whilst about twenty of the great courtiers and other dissolute persons were at basset round a large table, a bank of at least £2000 in gold before them, upon which two gentlemen who were with me made reflections in astonishment. Six days after, all was dust!"

But say what we may, there was something in the character, or at all events in the disposition of Charles which fascinated, and even continues to fascinate. It was not his personal appearance, for though tall and not ungraceful he was certainly not handsome. His rather cynical face was grim and his complexion swarthy, not at all that of "the merry monarch," which was the title bestowed upon him on account perhaps of his reputation for witty sayings and humorous retorts. Andrew Marvel says of him—

> "Of a tall stature and a sable hue,
> Much like the son of Kish, that lofty Jew;
> Ten years of need he suffer'd in exile,
> And kept his father's asses all the while."

The last line is a witty allusion to the occupation of Saul, and to the companions of Charles' banishment.

The king was a rapid and constant walker, and was by no means always the indolent lounger, gossiping with his mistresses, feeding his ducks, or playing with the spaniels which swarmed and littered in his apartments. After the fire of London, for instance, he was constantly about the streets, and underwent considerable fatigue encouraging, and frequently personally rewarding, the workmen engaged in clearing the ruins and in rebuilding the destroyed houses. One of the habits which endeared him to the people was the fearless familiarity with which he went amongst them, not only when the whole court, queen, courtiers, and mistresses, went out disposed for a frolic, but on ordinary occasions. In reference to his enthusiastic reception at the Restoration he had sarcastically remarked that it must have been his own fault he was so long absent, as every one seemed unanimous in promoting his return; but he continued to give practical effect to the expression of public confidence by walking about almost unattended. Dr. King says that once, when attended by only two noblemen, he met the Duke of York, who had been hunting on Hounslow Heath and was returning in his coach surrounded by his guards. The duke instantly alighted and expressed his fears that the king's life might be endangered by so small an attendance. "No kind of danger, James," said Charles; "for no man in England will take away my life to make you king."

This was an example of his witticisms, but they were always accompanied with that perfect courtesy, which, as we have already said, was his real charm, and this courtesy itself included a certain sense of social justice and good nature. Charles was too truly a gentleman to be personally vindictive, and even in his inconstancy there was some regard for what was due to his own code of honour. When Shaftesbury was compelled to deliver up his chancellorship, he begged the king to allow him to carry the seals once more, that he might not appear to be dismissed with contumely, and so might disappoint the crowd of his opponents who stood in the ante-chambers to witness his disgrace. "Oddsfish!" replied Charles, "I will not do it with any circumstance that looks like an affront;" and so, after a little of their usual gay conversation, the chancellor appeared as usual, and afterwards sent the seals to the king from his own private house.

It was to Shaftesbury that the king once said, "I verily believe thou art the wickedest dog in England." "For a *subject*, your majesty, I believe I am," retorted the profligate and witty statesman.

Charles once asked Stillingfleet why he always read his sermons in the Chapel Royal, but preached extempore everywhere else. Stillingfleet answered that it was from awe of his audience, and begged to ask why his majesty read his speeches to parliament. "Oddsfish! doctor," said the king, "'tis no difficult question. I always ask for money, and I have so often asked for it I am ashamed to look the members in the face."

There are several stories of his good-humoured satire, and some of them are very suggestive, such as that of the occasion when William Penn had an audience with his majesty, and in accordance with the custom of his sect kept his hat on. As a gentle rebuke Charles quietly took off his hat and stood uncovered before him. "Friend Charles," said Penn, "why dost thou not keep on thy hat?" "'Tis the custom of this place," replied the king, "for only one person to remain covered at a time."

If we are to accept the testimony of Dr. Birch it would seem that the king was at all events not always on the side of impiety and profanity; for he says that on one occasion the Duke of Buckingham having spoken profanely before him, Charles said, "My lord, I am a great deal older than your grace, and have heard more arguments for atheism; but I have since lived long enough to see that there is nothing in them, and I hope your grace will." On another occasion, speaking of the learned and credulous Vossius, who was a free-thinker, Charles said that "he refused to believe nothing but the Bible."

These and other anecdotes serve partly to explain the regard which his easy familiarity, associated with high-bred urbanity, obtained for Charles II.; but they afford no contradiction to that estimate of his character in which Macaulay represents him as having been distinguished for polite and engaging manners, and with some talent for lively conversation, but addicted beyond measure to sensual indulgence, fond of sauntering and of frivolous amusements, incapable of self-denial and of exertion, without faith in human virtue or in human attachment, without desire of renown or sensibility to reproach. "Honour and shame," says this historian, "were scarcely more to him than light and darkness to the blind. His contempt of flattery has been highly commended, but seems, when viewed in connection with the rest of his character, to deserve no commendation. It is possible to be below flattery as well as above it. One who trusts nobody will not trust sycophants. One who does not value real glory will not value its counterfeit."

This is harsh judgment, and should not be accepted without reflecting on the influences by which Charles' character were affected, his vicissitudes, the opposing interests to which he was subjected during his youth, and the fact that while it is less easy to form a just estimate of the character of a sovereign than of that of most other men, their lives are not only to a great extent open to public observation, but their biographies are written as frequently by bitter opponents as by subservient flatterers. At the same time the pages of Lord Macaulay's volumes are invaluable as brief chronicles of this period of English history, and especially that portion of them which relates to the state of England and the condition of the people in 1685.

THE EXECUTION OF LORD RUSSELL.

Among the leaders of that party which for a time successfully opposed the attempts of Charles II. and the Duke of York to re-establish arbitrary rule, and to favour the restoration of Romanism in England, one of the most prominent was Lord Russell, usually called Lord William Russell, son of William, Earl of Bedford, and Lady Ann Carr, daughter of Carr, Earl of Somerset.

Lord Russell, Lord Essex, Mr. Hampden, and Algernon Sidney were the principal supporters of the Exclusion Act, by which the Duke of York was not only compelled as a Papist to resign the admiralty, but would have been forbidden to ascend the throne. For a time they succeeded; but there arose a host of false accusers like Titus Oates and Dangerfield. Papist plots and Protestant plots were the subject of continual alarm and excitement, and the reign of persecution again set in. James, Duke of York, was sent to Scotland with plenary powers, which he used in putting Covenanters to the torture. Charles, without formally breaking the laws of the constitution, temporized, as it seemed, to discover how he might himself best profit by either party. Louis of France did his utmost to provoke anarchy by intriguing with all parties at the same time. A reaction came, which was greatly instigated by the violent measures taken against Roman Catholics by the Whig majority in the House of Commons.

The Duke of Monmouth, the illegitimate son of Charles, was one of the exclusionists, but was, it is supposed, too anxious to be on good terms with his father to keep his own counsel or to refrain from giving information which tended to the ruin of his friends. Shaftesbury was, if not the most violent, the most determined of the opponents of the claims of the Tories, and he declared that he could raise a force in the city, while Monmouth was to influence a rising in Cheshire and Lancashire, and Trenchard was to stir up the people of Taunton. The king and his counsellors had not been idle. Parliament was dissolved, and a new parliament in the royal interest was called at Oxford, where the Whigs had no influence. Charles demanded that he had the right of naming the sheriffs of London, and acting upon this false assumption, nominated two violent Tories, who were ready to support the royal prerogative. Men who spoke against the Duke of York were heavily mulcted. The infamous Jeffreys was recorder of London; the citizens, in fear of fines and executions, were divided amongst themselves; and the counteraction was complete when Shaftesbury, in despair of retrieving his position, threw up the cause of liberty and escaped to Holland, where a few weeks afterwards he died.

It now remained for Charles and his brother the Duke of York to strike at the party who were endeavouring to support the freedom of parliament and the rights of the constitution; and it was not difficult to do so, as some of its members were doubtless engaged in plans which might be called treasonable, though others, like Sidney and Russell, representing quite different opinions as to methods and results, were reformers who desired to act within the lines which the law gives to an assertion of public right.

In order to carry their plan into effect the reformers organized a select committee, called the "Council of Six." The members of this council were Monmouth, Essex (who was the chief adviser), Sidney, Russell, Lord Howard (introduced by Sidney), and young Hampden, a scholar and a grandson of *the* Hampden. What the deliberations of this council were it is now difficult to ascertain, owing to the prejudiced sources from which information has to be derived. There can be no doubt, however, that consultations were frequently held as to the best course to pursue for resisting a government which aimed at nothing less than arbitrary power. It is reported that the object of this council was to organize an insurrection all over the country, and, with the help of the discontented Presbyterians in Scotland, to put an end to the tyranny of Charles and his brother. What was the exact extent of these designs it is impossible to determine, unless we believe in the statements of Lord Grey and Bishop Sprat—the two most prejudiced and partial narrators of the Rye House Plot. In all probability there was, as Lady Russell said, much talk about a general rising, which "only amounted to loose discourse, or at most, embryos that never came to anything." She was convinced, she said, that it was no more than talk, "and 'tis possible that talk going so far as to consider, if a remedy to suppress evils might be sought, how it could be found."

Whilst the Council of Six were meditating their plans, whatever they might be, an inferior order of conspirators were holding meetings and organizing an insurrection perfectly unknown to the council. The chief of these conspirators were West, an active man, who was supposed to be an Atheist; Colonel Rumsey, an officer who had served under Cromwell, and afterwards in Portugal; Ferguson, an active agent of the late Lord Shaftesbury; Goodenough, who had been under-sheriff of London; Lieutenant-colonel Walcot, a republican officer; and several lawyers and tradesmen. The aim of these men seems to have been desperate and criminal in the extreme. They talked openly about murdering the king and his brother, and even went so far as to organize a scheme for that purpose. Among this band was one Rumbold, a maltster, who owned a farm called the Rye House, situated on the road to Newmarket, which sporting town Charles was accustomed to visit annually for the races. Rumbold laid before the conspirators a plan of this farm, and showed how easy it would be to intercept the king and his brother on their way home, fire upon them through the hedges, and then, when the deed of assassination was committed, escape by the by-lanes and across the fields. The murderous scheme of the maltster was, however, frustrated by Charles having been obliged to leave Newmarket eight days earlier than he had intended, owing to his house having taken fire. Treachery now put a stop to any further proceedings of the conspirators.

Among the minor persons engaged in the conspiracy was one Keeling, an Anabaptist, who, having failed as a salter, thought that as Oates and others had flourished so well in the trade of a witness, he might as well follow their example. He had been employed by Goodenough as a spy in the city, and was intimately acquainted with the movements and designs of the conspirators. Accordingly he went to Lord Dartmouth and told his tale, and was referred by his lordship to Mr. Secretary Jenkins. Jenkins took down his deposition, but said that unless his evidence was supported by another witness he could not proceed to the investigation of the matter. Keeling was, however, equal to the occasion, and induced his brother to corroborate his statements. The plot now authenticated by two witnesses, Jenkins thought it his duty to communicate the affair to the rest of the ministry. The younger Keeling, who had been compelled against his will to give evidence, secretly informed Goodenough that the plot had been discovered, and advised all engaged in it to flee beyond sea.

This news reaching Rumsey and West, who were inseparable allies, the two began to think it the safer policy to take a leaf out of the book of Keeling and reveal the whole plot—with a few additions. A house at Rye had been offered them by one Rumbold for the execution of their design. At this house forty men, well armed and mounted, commanded in two divisions by Rumsey and Walcot, were to assemble. On the return of the king from Newmarket, Rumsey with his division was to stop the coach and kill the king and the duke, whilst Walcot was to occupy himself in engaging with the guards. This done, they were to defend the moat till night, and then make their escape towards the Thames.

The details of the story once arranged, Rumsey and West had not to wait long before their veracity was put into requisition. Three days after Keeling's discovery the plot broke out, and was the talk of all the town. Examinations were freely taken, and many suspected persons seized. A proclamation having been issued to secure those who could not be found, Rumsey and West, whose names were mentioned in the proclamation, delivered themselves up to justice of their own accord. And now their story of the plot was at once divulged. In spite of the little difficulties and improbabilities it contained—such as the absence of any important person to head the insurrection, the awkward fact of only being able to name eight out of the forty armed men who were to assemble at Rye, the ignorance as to how arms and horses were to be supplied, the very practicable idea of defending themselves within mud walls and a moat, and the like—the story was implicitly believed. As an agreeable addition to this manufactured revelation the new witnesses declared that they had heard 'of the conferences that the Duke of Monmouth and the other lords had with those who were come from Scotland, but knew nothing of it themselves' (a very safe and cautious reserve). Rumsey, however, said that he remembered the meeting at Shepherd's and the talk about seizing the king's guards.[1]

In this critical situation Lord Russell, though perfectly sensible of his danger, acted with the greatest composure. He had long ago told a friend that he was very sensible he should fall a sacrifice. Arbitrary government could not be set up in England without wading through his blood. The day before the king arrived a messenger of the council was sent to wait at his gate to stop him if he had offered

---

[1] Ewald *Life and Times of Algernon Sidney*.

to go out; yet his back gate was not watched, so that he might have gone away if he had chosen it. Yet he thought proper to send his wife amongst his friends for advice. They were at first of different minds; but as he said he apprehended nothing from Rumsey, who had named him in his accusation, they agreed that his flight would look too much like a confession of guilt. This advice coinciding with his own opinion he determined to stay where he was. As soon as the king arrived a messenger was sent to bring him before the council. When he appeared there the king told him that nobody suspected him of any design against his person, but that he had good evidence of his being in designs against his government. He was examined upon the information of Rumsey. When the examination was finished Lord Russell was sent a close prisoner to the Tower. Upon his going in he told his servant Taunton that he was sworn against, and they would have his life. Taunton said he hoped it would not be in the power of his enemies to take it. Lord Russell answered, "Yes; the devil is loose!"

It is not necessary to enter into the points of the trial, which followed an examination by the privy-council. The bench had been supplied with accommodating judges. Jeffreys was one of the counsel for the prosecution; an illegally returned jury was not allowed to be challenged; the witnesses were perjured, contradicted themselves, and swore to save their lives. One of them (Lord Howard), who had previously declared that he knew nothing that could hurt Lord Russell, was a man of such infamous character that the king said he "would not hang the worst dog he had upon his evidence." Nevertheless his evidence was taken against the testimony of a number of honourable men.

The ground on which Lord Russell was sentenced to death was that he had violated the law in conspiring the death of the king. He argued that, granting the charge to be true (which he denied), it was not that of conspiring the death of the king, but "a conspiracy to levy war;" that this was not treason within the statute (which it was not); and that if it had been, a statute of Charles II. made the accusation null and void, because the time had expired to which the operation of it was limited.

His wife, Lady Rachel Russell, the daughter of the virtuous and noble Earl of Southampton, was his chief friend and counsellor. At

his trial, wishing to have notes of the evidence, he asked whether he might have somebody to write for him. The Chief-justice Pemberton said, "Any of your servants shall assist you in writing anything you please." "My lord," said Russell, "my wife is here to do it." And when the spectators turned their eyes and beheld the devoted lady rise up to assist her lord in this his uttermost distress, a thrill of anguish ran through the assembly.

Essex had been taken to the Tower, and while the perjured Howard was giving his evidence intelligence reached the court that in a fit of depression the noble lord had committed suicide. The attorney-general made use of the information to declare that Essex had killed himself to escape the hands of justice. The trial proceeded: the false witness, having recovered the shock of the dreadful news, went on with his evidence, and others swore to save their own lives. Before the jury withdrew Russell said to them, "Gentlemen, I am now in your hands eternally—my honour, my life, my all; and I hope the heats and animosities that are among you will not so bias you as to make you inclined to find an innocent man guilty. I call heaven and earth to witness that I never had a design against the king's life. I am in your hands; so God direct you!" But the jury soon brought in a verdict of guilty; and Treby, recorder of London, who had formerly been an exclusionist, and who had been deeply engaged with Lord Shaftesbury in most of the city schemes and plots, pronounced the horrible sentence of death for high treason.

Many efforts were made to obtain the royal pardon; but Charles was inexorable, even though £100,000 was offered him by his lordship's father the Duke of Bedford, through the French mistress the Duchess of Portsmouth. Russell's friends urged him to petition both the king and the Duke of York, and he complied by writing letters, which were of no avail. Lord Cavendish, his friend, offered to manage his escape by changing clothes and remaining at all hazards to himself; but Russell refused, and prepared to die with Christian piety. There are few more affecting accounts than that of the last hours of this nobleman, who seems to have been greatly beloved by all who knew him; while the conduct of his wife, who long survived him, and saw the downfall of the house of Stuart, is an admirable example of courage and devotion. She threw herself at the king's feet and pleaded with many tears the merit and loyalty of her father as an atonement for those errors with which honest, however mistaken, principles had seduced her husband. It is said that Charles refused her even a reprieve of six weeks, saying, "How can I grant that man six weeks, who, if it had been in his power, would not have granted me six hours?"

Finding all applications vain, Lady Russell collected courage and endeavoured by her example to strengthen the resolution of her unfortunate lord. He exhibited no fear of his sentence. "His whole behaviour," says Burnet, "looked like a triumph over death." He said he felt none of those transports that some good people felt; but he had a full calm in his mind, no palpitation at heart, nor trembling at the thoughts of death. He was much concerned at the cloud that seemed to be now over his country; but he hoped his death would do more service than his life could have done. He asked Burnet to assist him in suggesting the way in which he should draw up a paper to leave behind him at his death, and he was three days employed for some time in the morning to write out his speech. He ordered four copies to be made of it, all which he signed; and gave the original, with three of the copies, to his lady, and kept the other to give to the sheriff on the scaffold. He also wrote to the king, in which he asked pardon for everything he had said or done contrary to his duty, protesting he was innocent as to all designs against his person or government, and that his heart was ever devoted to that which he thought was his majesty's true interest. He added that though he thought he had met with hard measures, yet he forgave all concerned in it from the highest to the lowest, and ended hoping that his majesty's displeasure at him would cease with his own life, and that no part of it should fall on his wife and children. "The day before his death," says Burnet, "he received the sacrament from Tillotson with much devotion: and I preached two short sermons to him, which he heard with great affection; and we were shut up till towards the evening. Then he suffered his children that were very young, and some few of his friends, to take leave of him: in which he maintained his constancy of temper, though he was a very fond father. He also parted from his lady with a composed silence; and as soon as she was gone, he said to me, 'The bitterness of death is passed;' for he loved and esteemed her beyond expression, as she well deserved it in all respects. She had that command of herself so much, that at parting she gave him no disturbance."

The substance of the paper delivered to the sheriff was first a profession of his religion and of his sincerity in it: that he was of the Church of England, but wished all would unite together against the common enemy; that Churchmen would be less severe, and Dissenters less scrupulous. He owned he had a great zeal against Popery, which he looked on as an idolatrous and bloody religion; but that though he was at all times ready to venture his life for his religion or his country, yet that would never have carried him to a black or wicked design. No man ever had the impudence to move to him anything with relation to the king's life; he prayed heartily for him, that in his person and government he might be happy both in this world and the next. He protested that in the prosecution of the Popish plot he had gone on in the sincerity of his heart, and that he never knew of any practice with the witnesses. He owned he had been earnest in the matter of the exclusion, as the best way in his opinion to secure both the king's life and the Protestant religion, and to that he imputed his present sufferings; but he forgave all concerned in them, and charged his friends to think of no revenges. He thought his sentence was hard, upon which he gave an account of all that had passed at Shepherd's. From the heats that were in choosing the sheriffs he concluded that matter would end as it now did, and he was not much surprised to find it fall upon himself; he wished it might end in him. Killing by forms of law was the worst kind of murder. He concluded with some very devout ejaculations.

This is the synopsis of Lord Russell's paper as delivered to the sheriff; and immediately after the execution, to which he went with the greatest composure and religious fortitude, copies of the document were printed, and distributed all over London. The king and the duke, with their supporters, may well have felt that they had not triumphed after all, for this paper must have contributed greatly to the events which followed, and to the final release of the country from the Stuarts. Within six years after the execution of Lord Russell, James II., when leaving his throne, and, seeking for aid, had the meanness or the stupidity to apply to the aged Earl of Bedford for assistance. "My lord," said the fugitive king, "you are an honest man, have great credit, and can do me signal service." "Ah! sir," replied the earl, "I am old and feeble, but I once had a son." The king is said to have been so struck with this reply that he was silent for some minutes.

JAMES II.

Probably did more to hasten and confirm the liberty which the nation universally demanded than would have been achieved by a sovereign of a more engaging temper, and a greater talent for government. Converted to the Church of Rome from an obstinate Protestantism, which he had maintained while he was in exile, he became in England a Popish bigot, and it required all the firmness and adroitness of Charles to overcome the difficulties which his premature avowal of the Roman Catholic faith occasioned. He was constantly suspected, and very generally disliked while he was Duke of York, and the emphatic promises and declarations which he made to the representatives of both church and state on his accession to the throne, though for a time they deceived the nation, were so immediately contradicted by his actions, that he was ultimately consigned to contemptuous banishment.

Immediately after the death of Charles, James hastened to the council and addressed its members in the following words:—"My lords, before I enter any other business I think fit to say something to you. Since it hath pleased Almighty God to place me in this station, and I am now to succeed so good and gracious a king as well as so very kind a brother, it is proper for me to declare to you that I will endeavour to follow his example, and particularly in that of his great clemency and tenderness to his people. I have been reported to be a man fond of arbitrary power; but that is not the only falsehood which has been reported of me; and I shall make it my endeavour to preserve this government, both in church and state, as it is now by law established. I know the principles of the Church of England are favourable to monarchy, and the members of it have shown themselves good and loyal subjects, therefore I shall always take care to defend and support it. I know, too, that the laws of England are sufficient to make as great a monarch as I can wish; and as I shall never depart from the just rights and prerogative of the crown, so I shall never invade any man's property. I have often before ventured my life in defence of this nation, and shall go as far as any man in preserving it in all its just rights and liberties."

After his proclamation every one of these protestations was falsified. On the Sunday after his brother's burial James went to mass publicly and in royal state. The leading representatives of the party which had been opposed to him when he was Duke of York were received with significant coldness and even with reproaches. A full narrative of the Rye House plot was published under his authority, and in virulent language it stated that the king knew of 20,000 persons who had been engaged in the design; an assertion which was regarded as a menace by every prominent Whig in the country. Another paper was issued, giving an account of the conversion to the Romish faith of his first wife, the unhappy daughter of the high churchman Clarendon, and it soon became evident that a period of bitter persecution was about to commence in which both political and religious animosity would be used for outraging the liberties of the people.

Instead of waiting for the assembling of parliament, the king issued a proclamation for the levying of the customs and excise, a part of the royal revenue which had only been granted to Charles for his life. To this he was incited by the advice of the infamous Jeffreys, who was then lord chief-justice and to obtain some excuse for the stretch of prerogative addresses of loyalty and congratulation were procured from various influential public bodies. Even an act which on the ground of humanity should have been approved, was made the occasion of asserting arbitrary power. The large number of Papists and Dissenters who had been shut up in prison were released by the royal warrant in spite of the law which forbade the sovereign to exercise the dispensing power; and after events seemed to show that this, instead of being an act of clemency, was only an attempt to gain such a degree of toleration for Papists, that they, in conjunction with the Dissenters, might have their disabilities removed for the purpose of overthrowing the Anglican Church.

The degree of admiration and regard with which the memory of Charles II. was afterwards associated must surely have been increased by the detestation in which the character and conduct of his brother were held. Charles was profligate and witty, selfish and courteous, indifferent and not altogether cruel, perfidious and good-humoured, constantly seeking personal aggrandizement and self-indulgence, but too astute to imperil his crown by insisting on untimely demands. James was not much less profligate than Charles in the particular of matrimonial unfaithfulness, and he had the additional disadvantage of selecting plain and even positively ugly mistresses. His court was more dull, and outwardly more decorous, than that of his brother had been; for while he was himself an offender, he was constantly doing penance for his vices, bemoaning them and promising to reform. The profound selfishness of the Stuarts seemed to reach the lowest depth in him, and he had all that perverse, clumsy rudeness of speech that lost so many friends to Charles I., without any of the kingly manner which sometimes made it tolerable. His indifference to the sufferings of others reached to a degree of cruelty which enabled him to inflict horrible punishments on his foes, and to persecute to the death even old men and weak women and children, who, without guilty intention, had been associated with those who were his declared opponents. His perfidy was so marked and undisguised, that it almost took the form of courageous mendacity, and he so little understood either his own position or that of the nation that he lost his throne by being either obstinate or pusillanimous at the wrong times and on the wrong occasions.

Charles had been a palterer with France, and had degraded himself and the nation by taking bribes from Louis, and doing very little for them. James was the vassal of the French king, and would perhaps have done a great deal in return for the large subsidies which he unblushingly begged for and accepted, but that he had never been able to acquire the power to make any particular return, and could only use his efforts to remain neutral in Europe; which was all that Louis expected. England had begun to acquire internal independence, and even during the persecutions, the infamous mockery of justice, the judicial murders, the appalling perjuries and sham plots which may be said to have made the whole reign of James II. a sort of "bloody assizes," had begun to look for the blessings of constitutional government. Had it been otherwise he might have lost his head; instead of this he was regarded as being unworthy of so much public notice, and was suffered to steal away from the kingdom as one who had become too insignificant to close an era in the history of the country or to take any part in coming events.

ALICE LISLE.

The arbitrary temper with which James II. endeavoured to obtain a prerogative enabling him to dispense with parliaments, was associated with a meanness of disposition that the English people never could forgive. The persecuting spirit which is perhaps an inevitable consequence of such bigotry as his, was allied to a low desire to inflict cruel punishments even on those whose opposition to his will arose from circumstances or from convictions which any generous mind would have taken into account. Even in cases where there was only the suspicion of disaffection he was relentless, and it was regarded as a crime for anybody to exhibit compassion for the objects of his barbarous sentences.

It is no excuse for him that the frightful atrocities and utterly unjust sentences executed against obscure and often comparatively innocent victims, after the Monmouth rebellion, were by the orders of the brutal Jeffreys and of the blood-stained Kirke. James had made Jeffreys lord chief-justice that he might become his ready and implacable instrument; and Feversham, who was as incapable as a commander as he was heartless as a man, excited the contempt of both court and city by his indolence, his foppery, and his want of military skill; yet he was made Knight of the Garter and captain of the First Life Guards, as a reward for defeating the poor, unarmed, but bold and determined, rebels of Somerset and Wiltshire, who yet continued to oppose the regular troops after Monmouth himself had fled. It was in reality his officers, and chiefly the great man who was then known only as Lieutenant Churchill, but who afterwards made his name terrible in Europe as the Duke of Marlborough, who really held the command; but when Feversham was summoned to court he left in authority at Bridgewater a fierce and malignant ruffian, one Percy Kirke, whose worst vices had been developed in the fortress of Tangier, where he had played the tyrant not only against the wretched barbarians of the country, but against the inhabitants of the city, the Jews and his own soldiers, whom he pacified after floggings and imprisonment by permitting them to beat, rob, and insult the people whom they were supposed to protect.

All that even the wealthier victims who fell under the ban of Kirke could obtain, in return for large bribes, was permission to flee from the country. The ships which were bound for New England were crowded at this juncture with so many fugitives from Sedgmoor that there was great danger lest the water and provisions should fail. These abominable exactions, however, can scarcely be wondered at when we know that afterwards, during "the bloody assizes," the inhuman and corrupt Jeffreys, who himself trafficked in pardons, condemned 841 prisoners to transportation, that these wretched persons were distributed into gangs and bestowed on the courtiers or those who could obtain court favour, the conditions being that the convicts should be carried to one of the West India Islands as slaves, and that they should not be emancipated for ten years. It was estimated by Jeffreys that each of them would be worth on the average from £10 to £15 after all charges were paid. The wretched sufferers had to undergo all the miseries to which the negro slaves of later times have alone been exposed in the detestable traffic between Congo and Brazil.

This traffic, and that in bribes for pardons, was shared even by the ladies of the queen's household and by her majesty herself, and it is recorded that they exhibited a rapacity in the odious trade which leaves the name of Marie D'Este, the queen of James II., tainted with infamy. While her husband was a subject and an exile, shut out from public employment and in imminent danger of being deprived of his birthright, the suavity and humility of her manners conciliated the kindness even of those who abhorred her religion; but she changed for the worse under the influence of royal fortune, or it may be that the society and example of her husband deteriorated her character. In one of the satires of the time are these lines:—

> "When duchess, she was gentle, mild, and civil,
> When queen, she proved a raging, furious devil."

A less irregular and more cruel massacre than that at Bridgewater was determined on, and it was notified to the Lord Chief-justice Jeffreys, that he might expect the great seal of lord-chancellor as a reward for faithful and vigorous service. At Doncaster the bloody assizes commenced. The court was hung with scarlet. More than three hundred prisoners were to be tried, but Jeffreys made short work of them by letting it be understood that the only way to obtain pardon or respite, was to plead guilty. Two hundred and ninety-two were sentenced to death, and in Dorsetshire seventy-four were hanged. There were fewer prisoners at Exeter, for the rebellion had only just extended to the borders of Devonshire; but in Somersetshire, which was reserved to the last, the chief-justice, who seems to have had little or no opposition from his fellow-judges, appears to have revelled in carnage. He was drunk with cruelty and blood, shouted and roared with horrible hilarity in court, while he abused and taunted witnesses, and threatened and denounced the unhappy prisoners, to whom he applied vile epithets. Neither rank, age, nor sex, youth nor purity of character, were of any avail to protect the unhappy victims of his brutality; and he acted only as one could act who was certain of the royal favour. He boasted that he had hanged more traitors than all his predecessors together since the Conquest; and it is certain that the number of persons whom he put to death in one month and in one shire very much exceeded the number of all the political offenders who have been put to death in our island since the Revolution. The number of executions on this circuit alone was 320; and the accounts of some of the cases are sufficient to move alike our sympathy, our horror, and our indignation.

Perhaps one of the first which is recorded is the most illustrative of the immovable dogged cruelty of James, and the atrocious readiness with which Jeffreys was ready to give it effect. It was at Winchester that the commission was first opened. Hampshire had not been the theatre of war, but many of the vanquished rebels, like their leader, fled thither. Two of them, John Hickes, a Nonconformist minister, and Richard Nelthorpe, a lawyer who had been outlawed for taking part in the Rye House plot, had sought refuge in the house of a gentlewoman named Alice Lisle. This lady, who was very infirm and of advanced age, was the widow of John Lisle, who had sat in the Long Parliament and in the High Court of Justice in the days of the Commonwealth. He had been made a lord by Cromwell, and though the titles conferred by the Protector were not acknowledged after the Restoration they were often used in courtesy even by Royalists. Thus Mistress Lisle, who was related to several respectable and some noble families, and who was herself distinguished for the gentleness and courtesy of her manner, was commonly known as the Lady Alice. Even her high Tory neighbours deeply respected her for her loyalty and great humanity. The Lady Abergavenny and the Lady St. John both testified that she had been a favourer of the king's friends in their greatest extremities during the civil war, and, among others, of those ladies themselves.

Her son, so far from taking arms for Monmouth, had served in the royal army against the rebellion. It was well known that she had deeply regretted some of the violent acts in which her husband had borne a part, and, as she herself had often declared, had shed bitter tears for the death of Charles I. Her husband had fled from England and found an asylum in Switzerland at the Restoration, and he was one of those who, though in exile, met their death at the hands of assassins in the interest of Charles II. He was shot in the back on a Sunday as he was about to enter a church in Lausanne by one of two horsemen, who immediately shouted, "God save the King!" and galloped off —crossing the Swiss frontier into France, leaving their victim dead where he had fallen. Such had been the exemplary conduct of his wife while her husband's party was in power, and so gentle the aid she had rendered to Cavalier fugitives, that her husband's estate had been confirmed to her by the interposition of Clarendon.

This was the woman who, though she was so old and feeble that she could scarcely follow the charges brought against her, and so deaf that she was unable to hear the indictment, was dragged before a tribunal at which her condemnation had been already determined. The same womanly kindness which had led her to befriend the Royalists in their time of need would not suffer her to refuse food and a hiding-place to the two wretched men who had entreated her to befriend them. She took them into her house, set meal and drink before them, and showed them where they might rest. The next morning her dwelling was surrounded by soldiers. Hicks was found concealed in the malt-house, and Nelthorpe in the chimney. By doing so she was (according to the law) guilty of high treason. In this respect the law is less merciful to the person who conceals an alleged traitor than to the person who conceals a felon or a murderer; for the hiding of a murderer is not regarded as murder, and there always is a difference made between the committer of a felony and an accessory after the fact. This difference in the law, unjust and monstrous as it was, had been practically rectified by the necessity that every just and noble mind feels for approving that sentiment of humanity, which cannot consent to deliver up to death, or

refuse to give food and shelter to the rebel or the traitor who is in instant peril or in mortal agony.

And it is just to say, that during many generations no English government, save one, has treated with rigour persons guilty merely of harbouring defeated and flying insurgents. To women especially has been granted, by a kind of tacit prescription, the right of indulging, in the midst of havoc and vengeance, that compassion which is the most endearing of all their charms. Since the beginning of the great civil war numerous rebels, some of them far more important than Hicks or Nelthorpe, have been protected from the severity of victorious governments by female adroitness and generosity. But no English ruler who has been thus baffled, the savage and implacable James alone excepted, has had the barbarity even to think of putting a lady to a cruel and shameful death for so venial and amiable a transgression.[1]

Even the barbarous law, as it then stood, was strained to destroy Alice Lisle. She was sent to the bar before the trial of Hicks or Nelthorpe, and the jury, composed of the principal gentlemen of Hampshire, shrunk from the thought of sending her to the stake for an act of humanity and mercy. Jeffreys cursed and swore, bullied and threatened the reluctant witnesses, and broke out into furious revilings, when there seemed to be a probability of their giving evidence in the prisoner's favour. The Lady Alice, in her defence, represented that though she knew Hicks to be in trouble when she took him in, she neither knew nor suspected that he had been concerned in the rebellion. He was a divine, a man of peace, and it had never occurred to her that he could have borne arms against the government. She had supposed that he wished to conceal himself because warrants were out against him for field-preaching. This again gave Jeffreys occasion for a volley of abuse against Presbyterianism, Whigs, and Dissenters which lasted for an hour. In his summing up he repeated his denunciations, and reminded the jury that the husband of the prisoner had borne a part in the death of Charles I., a declaration of which no proof was given. The jury retired and remained for a long time in consultation. The judge grew impatient, and sent to tell them that if they did not instantly return he would adjourn the court and lock them up all night. They came to say that they doubted if the charge

[1] Macaulay.

had been proven. Jeffreys expostulated with them vehemently, and after another consultation they gave a reluctant verdict of "Guilty."

Sentence was pronounced on the following morning, that Alice Lisle was to be burned alive that very afternoon. This abominable decision aroused the indignation even of those who were most devoted to the crown, and whom James himself was desirous to propitiate. The clergy of Winchester Cathedral protested against the sentence, and the brutal chief-justice feared to risk a quarrel with these supporters of the Tory party. The execution was deferred for five days; and during that time the friends of the unfortunate lady besought the king to be merciful. Ladies of high rank pleaded with him in vain. Feversham, who perhaps was bribed, spoke in her favour; even Clarendon, the king's brother-in-law, tried to obtain a pardon or a mitigation of the sentence. All was useless. The utmost that could be obtained was that her sentence should be commuted from burning to beheading. She was put to death on a scaffold in the market-place of Winchester, and underwent her fate with serene courage, a martyr whose death aided to hasten the downfall of the tyrant who condemned her and the approach of liberty to the whole nation.

THE SEVEN BISHOPS.

While Roman Catholics were liberated from the comparative obscurity of exclusion, and were being appointed not only to military and civil, but even to collegiate and ecclesiastial offices, Puritans and "Nonconformists," and especially Presbyterians, both in England and Scotland, were being persecuted with increased animosity. Not under the tyranny of Laud had their condition been so deplorable as at that time. Many Dissenters were cited before the ecclesiastical courts. Others found it necessary to purchase the connivance of the agents of the government by presents of hogsheads of wine, and of gloves stuffed with guineas. It was impossible for the separatists to pray together without precautions such as are employed by coiners and receivers of stolen goods. The places of meeting were frequently changed. Worship was performed sometimes just before break of day, and sometimes at dead of night. Round the building where the little flock was gathered, sentinels were posted to give the alarm if a stranger drew near. Yet with all this care it was often found impossible to elude the vigilance of informers. Through many years the autumn of 1685 was remembered by the Nonconformists as a time of misery and terror. Yet in that autumn might be discerned the first faint indications of a great turn of fortune, and before eighteen months had elapsed the intolerant king and the intolerant church were eagerly bidding against each other for the support of the party which both had so deeply injured.[1]

Roman Catholics were admitted to office in contravention of the law, and were allowed and encouraged in the public exercise of their religion, but penal laws were in rigorous force against Independents, Quakers, Baptists, and especially Presbyterians. The king used every effort to produce an alliance between the English and the Romish Church. The Tories had supported him in almost every emergency: the church was deferential and never wavered in its assertions of loyalty, the parliament was comparatively submissive, and he took care so to organize a system of mingled promises and threats that he imagined it would be subservient. He was mistaken. Men who were not supposed to care much for religion were ready to relinquish their offices and emoluments rather than open the door for Popish domination. Parliament opposed him till he took the alternative of proroguing parliament. The Cavalier party were for the king, but they were against the Papacy. The whole Anglican priesthood were ready to suffer rather than yield. James subsided into dogged tyranny, and unable to make a coalition between the English and Roman Churches to the exclusion of all other sects, he determined to attempt the establishment of a general Declaration of Indulgence, which, by relieving the sufferings of Nonconformists and Presbyterians, would gain them to his side against the Anglican clergy, and enable him to elevate the Roman Catholics to power. At the same time he proceeded to annul by his sole authority a series of statutes, and abrogated all the acts which imposed a religious test as a qualification for any civil or military office.

[1] Macaulay.

There were not wanting signs that numbers of the oppressed and persecuted Puritans would not accept a relaxation of the rigours with which they had been treated as the price of their joining to elevate Popery against the Protestant Church, even though that church had been concerned in embittering their lives and in forbidding them that freedom of conscience which they were now promised. Happily there had for a long time been a moderate party in the Anglican Church, consisting of divines eminent alike for learning and consistency, who had felt kindly towards those who, while they dissented from them in matters of church government and in some points of doctrine, were yet regarded by them as Christian brethren. The great body of Dissenters and their most eminent representatives had no reason to love either king or church; but they loved the true liberty of England, and they loved true liberty of conscience. Only a section of the Nonconformists could ever be induced to thank the king for his concessions, and to make common cause with him. The rest, under the influence of men like Baxter, Home, Kiffin, and Bunyan, stood aloof.

Nearly a year passed during which unsuccessful efforts were made to cause the English clergy to yield. On the 27th of April, 1668, when public suspicion and alarm had reached their height, James published another Declaration of Indulgence, and on the 4th of May he commanded the Protestant clergy to read it in all their churches on two successive Sundays. The king's temper was arbitrary and severe. The proceedings of the Ecclesiastical Commission were as summary as those of a court-martial; whoever ventured to resist might in a week be ejected from his parsonage, deprived of his whole income, pronounced incapable of holding any other spiritual preferment, and left to beg from door to door. There was no time to form an extensive combination. The order in council was gazetted on the 7th of May. On the 20th the declaration was to be read in all the pulpits of London and the neighbourhood. It was not easy to collect in so short a time the sense even of the bishops.

At this conjuncture the Protestant Dissenters of London won for themselves a title to the lasting gratitude of their country. The time had come when it was necessary to make a choice; and the Nonconformists of the city, with a noble spirit, arrayed themselves side by side with the members of the church in defence of the fundamental laws of the realm. Baxter, Bates, and Howe distinguished themselves by their efforts to bring about this coalition; but the generous enthusiasm of the whole Puritan body made the task easy. Those Presbyterian and Independent teachers who showed an inclination to take part with the king against the Ecclesiastical Establishment received distinct notice, that unless they changed their conduct their congregations would neither hear them nor pay them. Deputations waited on several of the London clergy imploring them not to judge of the Dissenting body from the servile adulation which lately filled the *London Gazette*, and exhorting them, placed as they were in the van of this great fight, to play the men for the liberties of England and the faith delivered to the saints. The London clergy, then universally acknowledged to be the flower of their profession, held a meeting. After much uncertainty and debate Dr. Fowler, vicar of St. Giles, Cripplegate, Tillotson, Patrick, Sherlock, and Stillingfleet declared their determination not to read the declaration. A resolution by which all present also pledged themselves to one another not to read it was then drawn up, and was sent round the city, where it was speedily subscribed by eighty-five incumbents.

Meanwhile several of the bishops were anxiously deliberating as to the course which they should take. On the 12th of May a grave and learned company was assembled round the table of the primate at Lambeth. Letters were forthwith written to several of the most respectable prelates of the province of Canterbury, entreating them to come up without delay to London. As there was little doubt that these letters would be opened if they passed through the office in Lombard Street, they were sent by horsemen to the nearest country post-towns on the different roads. By the 17th, William Lloyd, bishop of St. Asaph; Kerr, bishop of Bath and Wells; Lake, bishop of Rochester; and Sir Jonathan Trelawney, bishop of Bristol, a baronet of an old and honourable Cornish family, had arrived, and on the following day a meeting was again held at Lambeth, where Tillotson, Tennison, Stillingfleet, Patrick, and Sherlock were present. Prayers were solemnly read before the consultation began. After long deliberation a petition embodying the general sense was written by the archbishop, Sancroft, with his own hand.

In substance nothing could be more skilfully framed than this memorable document. All disloyalty, all intolerance, was earnestly disclaimed. The king was assured that the church still was, as she had ever been, faithful to the throne. He was assured also that the bishops would, in proper place and time, as lords of parliament and members of the Upper House of Convocation, show that they by no means wanted tenderness for the conscientious scruples of Dissenters. But parliament had, both in the late and in the present reign, declared that the sovereign was not constitutionally competent to dispense with statutes in matters ecclesiastical. The declaration was therefore illegal; and the petitioners could not, in prudence, honour, or conscience, be parties to the solemn publication of an illegal declaration in the house of God and during the time of divine service. This paper was signed by the archbishop and by six of his suffragans, Lloyd of St. Asaph, Turner of Ely, Lake of Chichester, Kerr of Bath and Wells, White of Peterborough, and Trelawney of Bristol.

It was now late on Friday evening, and on Sunday morning the declaration was to be read in the churches of London. It was necessary to put the paper into the king's hands without delay. The six bishops set off for Whitehall. The archbishop, who had long been forbidden the court, did not accompany them. James directed that the bishops should be admitted. He had heard from his tool Cartwright that they were disposed to obey, and only required some modification in the form of the royal mandate. His majesty was therefore in good humour. When they knelt before him he graciously told them to rise, took the paper from Lloyd, and said, "This is my lord of Canterbury's hand." "Yes, sir, his own hand," was the answer. James read the petition; he folded it up and his countenance grew dark. "This," he said, "is a great surprise to me. I did not expect this from your church, especially from some of you. This is a standard of rebellion." The bishops broke forth into passionate expressions of loyalty; but the king, as usual, repeated the same words over and over. "I tell you this is a standard of rebellion." "Rebellion!" cried Trelawney, falling on his knees. "For God's sake, sir, do not say so hard a thing of us. No Trelawney can be a rebel. Remember that my family has fought for the crown. Remember how I served your majesty when Monmouth was in the West." "We put down the last rebellion," said Lake; "we shall not raise another." "We rebel!" exclaimed Turner; "we are ready to die at your majesty's feet." "Sir," said Kerr, in a more manly tone, "I hope that you will grant to us that liberty of conscience which you grant to all mankind." Still James went on declaring that it was rebellion, that no good churchman had questioned the dispensing power before, that some

of the petitioners had preached for it and written for it, that he would have his declaration published. "We have two duties to perform," answered Kerr, "our duty to God and our duty to your majesty. We honour you, but we fear God." "Have I deserved this?" continued James, more and more angry, "I who have been such a friend to your church? I will be obeyed. My declaration shall be published. What do you do here? Go to your dioceses and see that I am obeyed. I will keep this paper. I will not part with it. I will remember you that have signed it." "God's will be done!" said Kerr. "What's that?" said the enraged king. "God's will be done!" repeated the bishops, who then respectfully retired.

That very evening the document which they had put in the hands of the king appeared in print—was laid on the tables of the coffee-houses, and was cried about the streets. How the petition got abroad is still a mystery. Sancroft declared that he had taken every precaution against publication, and that he knew of no copy except that which he had himself written, and which James had taken out of Lloyd's hand. The veracity of the archbishop is above suspicion. It is, however, not improbable that some of the divines who assisted in framing the document may have remembered so short a composition, and may have sent it to the press.

On the Sunday only seven out of 100 clergymen in the London parish churches read the declaration, while those who did so were groaned at by the people, who left the churches where the hated mandate was brought forward. The spirit of dissent seemed to be extinct. Baxter from his pulpit pronounced an eulogium on the bishops and parochial clergy. Another week passed away, and on the Sunday the churches were again crowded, but the declaration was nowhere read, except where it had been read the week before.

Even the king stood aghast for a moment at the violence of the tempest that he had raised. What step was he next to take? Should he cite them before the Ecclesiastical Commission, where Jeffreys was sole judge? Jeffreys shrank from such a responsibility, and recommended a criminal information. It was accordingly resolved that the archbishop and his six suffragans should be brought before the King's Bench on a charge of seditious libel before judges and officers who were creatures of the court, and would probably condemn them to fines and imprisonment, to escape which they would be glad to serve the designs of the king. First, however, they were cited to appear before the privy-council. Perhaps James thought that they might yet instruct their clergy to obey his order; but nothing of the kind took place. Not one parish priest in fifty consented to read. The Bishops of Norwich, Gloucester, Salisbury, Winchester and Exeter had signed copies of the petition in token of their approbation.

On the 8th of June the seven bishops were summoned before the privy-council. At first James and his Lord-chancellor Jeffreys affected a gracious manner to cajole them into submission, but they were firm. Sancroft acknowledged his hand-writing on the repeated demand of the king, and the others followed in owning the petition, with the proviso that they were not bound to admit anything which should be used against them. On Jeffreys demanding that they should enter into recognizances to appear and take their trial at Westminster Hall, they refused, on the ground that as peers they were not bound by recogniz- ances in misdemeanours. A warrant was then made out to commit them to the Tower.

Never since the first introduction of the mitre was Episcopacy so popular as on that day. "The concern of the people," says Evelyn, "was wonderful—infinite crowds on their knees, begging their blessing and praying for them as they passed. They were conveyed from Whitehall by water, and as they took boat they were followed by the tears and prayers of thousands, and men ran after them into the water to implore their blessing." The very soldiers at the Tower followed the general impulse; the sentinels who were under arms at the Traitor's Gate reverently asked a blessing from their prisoners; in the evening the men of the garrison were all drinking the health of the bishops, and the officers could not prevent it. All day the coaches and liveries of the first nobles of England were seen round the prison gates. Thousands of persons assembled on Tower Hill, and to the rage and alarm of the king a deputation of ten Nonconformist ministers waited on and condoled with the prisoners. James sent for four of these men and upbraided them. They answered that they thought it their duty to forget past quarrels and to stand by the men who stood by the Protestant religion.

The trial was adjourned on the first appearance of the bishops, and they were suffered to go to their own homes. On the 29th of June the bishops again entered Westminster Hall, surrounded by lords and gentlemen, and followed by blessings and prayers. James made sure of a verdict, for he thought the judges were his slaves, and that the jury would be subservient. But there were present men before whom even the lord chief-justice was abashed. "He looked," said a by-stander, "as if every peer had a halter in his pocket." The bishops were ably defended by some of the most capable lawyers of the day, and by Mr. Justice Powell, who was not to be put down by the clamour and bullying of the prosecution. The jury, of which Sir Robert Langley was foreman, was composed of respectable men, and in truth any jury would at that time have been more afraid of the people than of the king.

The trial lasted from nine in the morning till seven in the evening. The jury retired to consider their verdict, and were locked up all night —one Arnold, the king's brewer, holding out to the last. At length, however, he was overruled, and at nine o'clock the next morning, when the court was opened, Sir Robert Langley pronounced the verdict of "*Not guilty*." The next moment Lord Halifax waved his hat, and there arose such a mighty shout in the court that it was heard outside, and spread from Westminster to Temple Bar, whence it rolled in loud huzzas as far as the Tower, where the guard had been doubled.

All over London the people were laughing, crying, praying, and cheering with delight. The bishops as they walked to their barges exhorted their countrymen to fear God and honour the king. At night London was lighted from one end to the other with blazing bonfires, seven candles appeared in almost every window, all the church-bells were set ringing, and the pope was burned in effigy before the windows of the palace at Whitehall, while in several other places similar effigies were shown and ignited, much to the scandal of the papal nuncio and the rage of the king. The whole metropolis was in an uproar of congratulation, and horsemen were on every highroad to carry the welcome intelligence to the shires.

The Sunday had dawned and the bells of the parish churches were ringing for early prayers before the fires began to languish and the crowds to disperse. A proclamation was speedily put forth against the rioters. Many of them, mostly young apprentices, were apprehended, but the bills were thrown out at the Middlesex sessions. The magistrates, many of whom were Roman Catholics, expostulated with the grand-jury, and sent them back three or four times, but to' no purpose.

Immediately after the verdict the attorney took the tidings to Sunderland. The king was at the camp at Hounslow Heath, and Sunderland sent a courier with the news. James was in Lord Feversham's tent, and when he received the message was greatly disturbed, exclaiming in French, "So much the worse for them." While he was present, respect and discipline prevented any demonstration on the part of the soldiers; but he had scarcely quitted the camp when he heard a great shouting behind him, and turning in surprise asked what it meant. "Nothing," was the answer. "The soldiers are glad that the bishops are acquitted." "Do you call that nothing?" said James; and then he repeated, "So much the worse for them."

ENGLAND'S NEW ERA.

Long before the flight of James, and the departure of his queen with the infant prince whose alleged birth a large number of the people had persisted in representing as an imposture, the attention of the whole nation had been directed to William Henry, prince of Orange Nassau, the acknowledged defender of Protestantism in Europe, and the husband of Mary, eldest daughter of James and his first wife Anne Hyde.

William was the posthumous son of William II. of Orange, and Mary, daughter of Charles I. His father was the eldest son of the Stadtholder Frederic Henry, who was the youngest son of William the Silent, and Louisa, daughter of the famous Admiral Coligny. Thus the future King of England was cousin and husband to the heiress to the English throne, and was also directly descended from the great founder of the Dutch Republic and from the renowned leader of the Huguenots.

William of Orange was an orphan in early childhood—a fatherless and motherless boy—virtually the chief of a great party which was for the time depressed by the oligarchy which, under the influence of the De Witts, then ruled the United Provinces. That the child was heir to the great office of stadtholder, and the descendant of its most illustrious representative, was sufficient reason for his being held in the position of a state prisoner, whose every word and action needed to be watched, and whose appearance in public was to be discouraged because of the enthusiasm of the people for his house and name. It is little wonder that a childhood so passed should have so operated on a firm nature as to increase a natural reserve to habitual reticence, and to make a temper not prone to elasticity often grim and repellent. There was so little opportunity for the cultivation of sympathy that we may cease to wonder at the unconciliatory habit of the prince, who was yet capable of deep and sincere attachments. He was scarcely fifteen years old when all the domestics who were loyal to his interests, or who enjoyed any share of his confidence, were removed from under his roof. His health, never robust, would have sunk from a sense of his desolate position, but that he had both the courage and the sagacity which had distinguished his ancestors. Long before he reached manhood he knew how to keep secrets, how to baffle curiosity by dry and guarded answers, how to conceal all passions under the same show of grave tranquillity. He perhaps emulated the reserve of William the Silent, who trusted nobody with his intentions till they were being executed, and who, when one of his most influential companions once asked him what would be his line of conduct in an approaching crisis, said, "Can you keep a secret?" "Implicitly," replied the anxious inquirer. "So can I," returned the imperturbable stadtholder, and so closed the conversation.

The education of William of Orange, like his tastes, was of a practical and severe kind. He possessed few or no accomplishments, sought no grace of manner. He was blunt even for a Dutchman of that period, and though he spoke and wrote French, and probably understood it well, his letters in that language were remarkably crude both in composition and spelling. He also understood Latin, Italian, and Spanish, for these languages were necessary to a man who had to answer both in speaking and writing questions involved in the great political events of Europe. Of course he wrote and spoke English fluently and intelligibly, though not elegantly, but he never thoroughly understood the English people, and during his lifetime they neither understood nor sympathized with him except when they discovered the intensity of feeling which could move that apparently cold impassive nature, on the death of the English wife whom he profoundly loved, and who had been so devoted to him as to yield, without a second thought, the crown which they shared together, but which was hers by right of inheritance.

Not only the early education, but the great position of William of Orange as the defender of the Protestant religion, and as the general and statesman who had set himself to the task of thwarting, of defying, and ultimately of humbling France, directed his vigorous intellect only to those studies which were necessary to a complete knowledge of public affairs, of political administration, and of military tactics. Neither literature nor science claimed much attention from him; of poetry he seemed to know nothing; the drama tired him; he was neither wit nor orator, though he could utter sharp sarcasms, and could speak with vigour and to the purpose when occasion demanded it. Except amidst that inner circle of intimate friends of whom his loved companion the faithful Bentinck was the most conspicuous, his social qualifications appeared to be few and ungenial; but those who knew him intimately, discovered that there was a real tenderness and a simple pleasantry in the man, which, when once the ice of his cold caution and silent self-control was broken, revealed unsuspected depths of feeling. The familiar letters which he wrote to his friend attest not only his simplicity of heart, but his unaffected regard and gratitude for those true services which princes are often apt to forget.

Perhaps one reason for the unmoved and cautious exterior which he maintained may be found in the fact that on occasions he was liable to sudden outbursts of anger which startled those who encountered them, and appeared to be the more furious because they were volcanic fires that burst from beneath a thick crust of ice. But for any injustice of which William was guilty during an outburst of temper he was so penitent and so anxious to compensate, that it is said he not only disarmed the indignation of the noble-minded, but almost excited the cupidity of those who would even venture to brave his wrath for the sake of the amends which he might make. But his self-control was too great to make this a frequent occurrence, and it was in war that the natural outbreak of his force of character found occasion to display itself. Indeed his personal tastes were those rather of a warrior than of a statesman; but he, like his grandfather,

the silent prince who founded the Batavian commonwealth, occupies a far higher place among statesmen than among warriors. He was almost always opposed to those who were consummate masters of the art of war, and to troops far superior in discipline to his own, and this may be sufficient to account for the fact that he was not successful: but he could not lay claim to being a great general, for he had received no military education, had been placed while yet a boy at the head of the army, and could only learn by the experience which comes of failure. He himself once declared that he would give a good part of his estates to have served a few campaigns under the Prince of Condé before he had to command against him, and yet the great Condé with generous admiration remarked, after the bloody day of Seneff, that the Prince of Orange had in all things borne himself like an old general, except in exposing himself like a young soldier.

Indeed the personal courage and cool disregard of danger which distinguished William must have contributed greatly to the marvellous alacrity with which he was able, though not victorious, to retrieve defeat, or the determined persistency with which he maintained an advantage. If his battles were not those of a great tactician, they entitled him to be called a great man. No disaster could for one moment deprive him of his firmness or of the entire possession of all his faculties, nor did his adverse fortune ever lose him of the respect and confidence of his soldiers. That respect and confidence he owed in a great degree not only to the bravery which is necessary to carry a soldier through an arduous campaign, but to a rarer sort of courage which in his case was proved by almost every test—by war, by wounds, by painful and depressing maladies, by raging seas, by the imminent and constant risk of assassination, a risk which has shaken very strong nerves, a risk which severely tried even the adamantine fortitude of Cromwell. Yet none could ever discover what that thing was which the Prince of Orange feared. His advisers could with difficulty induce him to take any precautions against the pistols and daggers of conspirators, even when the Jacobites of St. Germains were constantly contriving schemes of assassination. He not only received the intimations of these dangers without disturbance, but with cold magnanimity refused to investigate them or to punish their originators until their plans became dangerous to the nation itself.

It cannot be denied, however, that though William was neither tyrannical nor revengeful, he had that kind of arbitrary disposition which would brook no rival assumptions, and this is not much to be wondered at when his early difficulties and his subsequent necessary assumption of authority are considered. He was no persecutor, and had no mean desire to avenge small injuries, but he did not display that noble generosity of temper that only belongs to the highest class of men. He was certainly not cruel, but he could regard the horrors of war and punish by fire and sword with an equanimity which, regarding it as the necessary means for maintaining his government and checking what might be serious opposition to his plans, appeared to be undisturbed by those considerations of humanity that belong alike to smaller and to greater men.

It must be remembered, however, that he had so learned to control every manifestation of feeling for the purpose of keeping his own counsel against those who sought to discover and to thwart his designs, that it was difficult to read any emotion beneath his imperturbable manner. The massacre of Glencoe, the atrocity and treachery of which aroused the feelings of the whole nation, was probably from this cause scarcely denounced by William with the same natural expressions of indignation which moved the general sympathy, and though there is sufficient reason to believe that he was wholly unacquainted with that horrible event till after it was effected, he has since been charged with it as a part of that cold-blooded policy which his enemies attributed to him.

As warrior and statesman William brought to England a new era of history at a period when a determined courage, an inflexible will, and a just and yet liberal policy were essential to prevent a restoration which would have been a death-blow to national honour and freedom, or a revolution which would have resulted in a devastating civil war.

The remarkable strength of character which distinguished William of Orange was not allied to a strong physical frame. His favourite recreation was the chase, and he loved it most when it was most hazardous. His leaps were so daring that his boldest companions hesitated to follow him. By a remarkable contrast, though he endeavoured in his grander palace and his finer grounds and gardens in England to reduce everything to the inartistic Dutch formality of his gardens at Loo, he also pined for the excitement which had delighted him in hunting wolves, wild-boars, and great stags in the forest of Guelders.

Yet his physical organization was unusually weak. As a child he had been sickly. In the prime of manhood his complaints had been aggravated by a severe attack of small-pox, through which his friend Bentinck had attended him with faithful affection. He was asthmatic and consumptive. His slender frame was shaken by a constant hoarse cough. He could not sleep unless his head was propped up by pillows. Through a life which was one long disease the force of his mind never failed on any great occasion to bear up his suffering and languid body. "His name," says Macaulay, who is one of his chief panegyrists, "at once calls up before us a slender and feeble frame, a lofty and ample forehead, a nose curved like the beak of an eagle, an eye rivalling that of an eagle in brightness and keenness, a thoughtful and somewhat sullen brow, a firm and somewhat peevish mouth, a cheek pale, thin, and deeply furrowed by sickness and care, that pensive, severe, and solemn aspect could scarcely have belonged to a happy or a good-humoured man. But it indicates in a manner not to be mistaken capacity equal to the most arduous enterprise, and fortitude not to be shaken by reverses or dangers."

Mary, who must have recognized in her husband a character lofty indeed when contrasted with that of her uncle or her father, was entirely devoted to him. A woman with no small share of personal beauty, a dignified carriage, admirable truth and sweetness of disposition, and a large share of sound common sense and unaffected piety, she loved him so well that she even pardoned that passing unfaithfulness which, on more than one occasion, William, in common with every prince of the time, showed to the claims of marriage, and sought to win him by an amiability which she evidently regarded as a part of her religion.

That she succeeded is evident from the close affection with which he regarded her—an affection more distinctly manifested, it is true, after she had declared to him that if she succeeded to the throne of England she should yield to him the crown, and observe the Scripture precept, "Wives, obey your husbands," in the hope that he too would obey that which said, "Husbands, love your wives." But William had never hinted to her the dissatisfaction with which he looked forward to the probability of playing a second part under his wife's rule; and but for the shrewdness of Bishop Burnet, who guessed at the cause of William's moody silence, and communicated it to the princess, she would not have been able to delight him so soon by this fresh proof of her affection, which entirely gained his heart, if it was not already hers.

Mary, in common with her sister Anne, who remained in England with her husband Prince George of Denmark, has been charged with a want of filial regard and with base disloyalty in contemplating the abdication of her father, and aiding in his continued banishment. On the other hand, we must reflect that they were daughters of the first wife of James, were both Protestants, and that their father had not regarded their claims to succession, when, by his determined efforts to establish Popery, he imperilled both the crown and the nation: that the husband of Mary was the head of the Protestant cause in Europe, and himself allied to the royal family of England, and that he was the only man to whom the people of this country could look to deliver them from the detested rule of a weak king whom they both feared and despised, or from the invasion of a foe who had supported the tyranny under which they writhed.

To the great resentment of James, Bishop Burnet, whom he regarded as one of his bitterest enemies, had occupied the position of private secretary at the Hague, and even when, in deference to his father-in-law's demands, William dispensed with his services, he was still a confidential adviser, whose knowledge of English parties and English character was derived from long acquaintance with the leading men of this country.

The representative of Holland at the English court was Dykvelt, in whom skill as a diplomatist and dexterity of temper and manners were added to a remarkable knowledge of English affairs. It was William's desire to unite the Protestant parties in one common determination, and no one was better fitted to effect this coalition than Dykvelt, whose embassy was in fact less to the government than to the opposition. For both the Prince and Princess of Orange, while speaking favourably of a considerable mitigation of religious tests and disabilities, had firmly refused to support the Declaration of Indulgence and the promotion of Roman Catholics to offices of state. "You ask me," said William to one of the king's agents, "to countenance an attack on my own religion. I cannot with a safe conscience do it, and I will not, no, not for the crown of England, nor for the empire of the world." Both he and his wife were convinced

that James had usurped a prerogative that did not belong to him, and seriously advised him to govern in all things according to law. Against usurpation they protested not only as friends to civil liberty, but as members of the royal house who had a deep interest in maintaining the rights of the crown, for experience had shown that in England arbitrary government could not fail to produce a reaction even more pernicious than itself.

Nothing would arrest the mad folly of James, though he saw that Dykvelt was mustering the divisions of the opposition. The great chiefs Danby, Nottingham, Halifax, and several of the eminent Whigs were stirring for action, Bishop Compton was influencing the clergy, Admiral Herbert the navy, and an interest was established in the army by the instrumentality of Churchill, whose wife (formerly Sarah Jennings) was the confidante and intimate friend of the Princess Anne. His sister had been the mistress of the king, and he, once a needy ensign, was now, in his thirty-seventh year, a major-general, a peer of Scotland, commander of a troop of Life Guards, and the holder of several considerable offices. A change must have appeared imminent indeed when that cold-hearted, avaricious, and self-contained man declared in favour of the maintenance of Protestantism, and as it would seem with a real horror of having either to relinquish his lucrative posts, or of abjuring a religion which he dared not forsake, little as his life and character may have been in accordance with it.

The general feeling against the king may be indicated by the wide-spread acceptance of the report that the reputed heir to the throne was really no child of his, but had actually been introduced into the queen's chamber. The popular fancy decided on the means of conveyance having been a warming-pan; and it was hinted that the alleged expectation of an heir was a pretence, while the alleged birth of the child during the absence of the Princess Anne and of some other notable Protestant personages was regarded as a part of the imposture. That a sufficient number both of Protestants and Romanists were present to verify the birth of the child there can be little doubt. The officiating surgeon on the occasion was the famous Dr. Chamberlain, who was not only a Protestant but a noted Whig, and one who had suffered some persecution. James himself caused to be examined on oath about forty persons, whose evidence may be regarded as conclusive. Still the people would not accept the testimony, and Anne joined in representing to William and her sister that there was a doubt as to the birth of a prince.

William, whether he believed the report or not, had begun to make preparations for an actual invasion of England. Count Zuleystein, who had been sent as ambassador from the States to congratulate James, returned with a formal invitation from a great number of noblemen and gentlemen for the Prince of Orange to come over with an armed force to call the legitimacy of the child in question, and to redress the grievances of the nation. The former was unnecessary, the latter William had determined to do if the nation itself ultimately demanded it. A regular intercourse was opened between London, Edinburgh, Dublin, and the Hague, and men of name, wealth, and influence joined in the request for the Prince of Orange to come at once.

By the month of August he had collected 15,000 land troops, a train of artillery, seventy vessels and flat-bottomed boats to effect a landing, and observing his usual impenetrable silence, kept the enterprise a secret from all but five or six persons in his confidence. Louis of France thought that he was meditating an attack either on his ally the King of Denmark or on the Dutch republicans. James fancied that he was preparing for hostilities with France. When it was too late both of them found out what the preparations meant; and James made some offers of concession and retractation, in which few people believed, though he consulted the bishops, replaced some Protestant deputy-lieutenants and magistrates, gave back its charter to the city, and spoke respectfully of parliament as the best means of settling difficulties.

On Friday the 16th of October William embarked with some of his own noblemen and generals, and many English noblemen. His ship bore the flag of England and his own arms, with the motto, "I will maintain the Protestant religion and the liberties of England." The fleet was at first scattered by adverse winds, and had to put into Helvoet with some damage, but on the 1st of November it sailed a second time. The English fleet, which had suffered by the storm, could not get away from the Downs, but it is doubtful if the men would have fought, and the Dutchmen came to anchor at Torbay on the 4th of November, the anniversary of William's birth and of his marriage with the Princess Mary. On the 5th of November, the anniversary of the Gunpowder Plot, he landed, and immediately marched to Exeter with about 15,000 men, of whom 2000 were English, Scotch, and Irish Protestants. Everywhere there was disaffection—many of the principal towns were declaring for the prince, whole regiments with their officers were deserting the royal cause,—the city of London was in riotous disorder.

A council of war was called at Whitehall, and the king was advised at once to call a parliament—an entreaty in which the bishops joined —and to proceed at once to the head-quarters of the army at Salisbury. The little Prince of Wales was sent to Portsmouth for safety; monks and priests were already in flight. James set out with the French ambassador Barillon, but in five days returned to London, retreating from the wide-spread defection which left him little hope of retrieving his position. Stopping at Andover on his way back, he invited Prince George of Denmark (his son-in-law) and the Duke of Ormond to sup with him. The very next morning they were both missing, and had gone straight from the royal table to join the Prince of Orange. George, who had little to say for himself, and was a dull fellow, who enjoyed his dinner and his bottle without troubling himself much with public affairs, had used one stock phrase when he heard of the desertion of any of James' former friends. He expressed at once his surprise and his sympathy by ejaculating, "*Est-il possible?*" When the king found that he also had deserted him he said with a bitter sense of humour, which was perhaps the nearest approach he ever made to the wit of Charles, "*Est-il possible* gone too!" Still more sad was the discovery on reaching Whitehall that Anne had also absconded with Lady Churchill.

William and his troops were joyfully expected at Oxford. The Papist court was emptying fast. Proclamations were useless, proposals for negotiation with the Prince of Orange were of no avail, promises of amendment and the issue under the Great Seal of a general pardon to offenders, had no effect. There was nothing for it but for the king himself to take to flight. After having reached Sheppey, where he was compelled to seek the protection of Lord Winchelsea, he returned to London, much to the surprise of William, who was at Windsor, earnestly desiring that his father-in-law might get quietly away to France; and also to the surprise of the provisional council, who had sent Lord Feversham to him with 200 Life Guards as an escort, and a polite message to ask if he would come back to London or continue his journey. He was eventually induced to go to Rochester, whence he embarked in a fishing smack, passed the ships at the Nore unchallenged, and landed at Ambleteuse. Thus,—

> "Prick'd by the Papal spur, we rear'd,
> We flung the burthen of the Second James."

The "Glorious Revolution"—which was truly glorious in its results, though the treachery, falsehood, and cowardice of many of those who were concerned in it are so depressing—was not completed by the flight of the king. Two months elapsed before Whigs and Dissenters, Tories and High Churchmen, came to an agreement.

The Prince of Orange had taken up his residence, not at Whitehall but at St James', and scrupulously avoided either interposition or the assumption of any right. On the 25th of December about ninety lords, spiritual and temporal, who had resumed their places in the House of Lords, requested him to take upon himself the administration of affairs and the disposal of the public revenue, and to issue writs for a "Convention," to meet on the 22d of January. On the following day an assembly of 150 persons, who had sat in parliament in the reign of Charles II., together with the aldermen of London and fifty of the common council, met at St James' at the request of the prince, and thence proceeded to the Commons House and agreed to an address similar to that of the Lords. The prince then despatched circular letters to the several counties, universities, cities, and boroughs, and in the meantime the country, the fleet, and what remained of James' army, submitted quietly to the new rule. In Ireland it was very different; but in Scotland men were as prompt in their obedience as in England.

On the 22d of January the convention (afterwards named the parliament), set about its work in earnest. A letter from William was read in both houses. His highness told them he had endeavoured to the utmost of his power to perform what had been desired of him, in order to maintain the public peace and safety; that it now rested with themselves to lay the foundation of a firm security for their religion, their laws, and their liberties. In the Commons there was a vast enthusiasm, and the Lords were not backward in expressions of satisfaction. They appointed a day of thanksgiving to Almighty God for having made his highness the glorious instrument of the great deliverance of the kingdom from Popery and arbitrary power; and they joined the Commons in an address of thanks to the prince, which said,

"And we do most humbly desire your highness to take upon you the administration of public affairs, and the disposal of the public revenue for the preservation of our religion, rights, laws, liberties, and properties, and of the peace of the nation."

William delayed an answer till the next day, when he laconically said, "My lords and gentlemen, I am glad that what I have done hath pleased you; and since you desire me to continue the administration of affairs, I am willing to accept it." The two houses then adjourned to the 28th, when the next serious decision had to be come to. There was a long and stormy debate before the resolution was passed, "that King James II., having endeavoured to subvert the constitution by breaking the original contract between king and people, and by the advice of Jesuits and other wicked persons having violated the fundamental laws and withdrawn himself out of the kingdom, has abdicated the government, and that the throne is thereby become vacant." The next day it was voted "that it hath been found by experience to be inconsistent with the safety and welfare of this Protestant kingdom to be governed by a Popish prince." The debate in the Lords on the former resolution was sharp and protracted, and a regency was proposed, while the maintenance of hereditary succession was also advocated; but at last yielding to the force of circumstances, it was resolved that the Prince and Princess of Orange should be declared King and Queen of England and all the dominions thereunto belonging.

The final resolution to which both houses came on the 12th of February, 1689, was, that William and Mary should be declared King and Queen of England, France, and Ireland, and the dominions thereunto belonging; with the sole and full exercise of the regal power during their joint lives; that the succession should be to the issue of the said princess, or failing her issue to the Princess Anne of Denmark, and her issue, or failing them to the heirs of the body of the Prince of Orange. On the same day Mary arrived from Holland at Whitehall, and on the morrow the prince and she being seated in the banqueting-house, both houses of the convention waited upon them with the declaration and resolution of the two houses, which was read by the clerk of the crown, the Marquis of Halifax making a solemn tender of the crown to their highnesses; and on the same day, being Ash Wednesday, William and Mary were proclaimed king and queen, amidst general acclamation and rejoicing.

THE BATTLE OF LA HOGUE.

On the 25th of November, 1690, William told the convention, which had been transformed into a parliament, that the position of affairs abroad imperatively required his presence at the Hague, in order to direct the counsels and to consolidate the action of the confederacy, which was again preparing to oppose the assumptions of France. It was necessary to grant a large sum of money that England might take her proper place in the defence of her own liberties, and in protecting other states from the encroachment of the common enemy. The parliament responded by voting £4,000,000 for an army of 60,000 and a navy of 28,000 men—the largest grant that had ever been made in England; and they afterwards voted another £500,000 for building new ships of war.

The king was eminently successful in arousing the energies of the confederacy; but before he could rally his allies in Flanders to raise the siege of Mons, that city had capitulated, and he returned to England to get the British fleet to sea, under the command of Admiral Russell, who, though not far from being a republican by theory, was in secret communication with St. Germains, and if not actually a traitor was strongly suspected of half-heartedness. The king returned to the Continent, and at the head of about 70,000 men protected Brussels from the operations of the French army under Marshal Luxembourg, who was compelled to retire in order to avoid an action, which he only escaped by marching and countermarching his troops. William left the command to Prince Waldeck, and returned to England to ask parliament for further supplies; but the opposition, consisting of those who had not been appointed to offices of state, for a time set themselves against further grants. Eventually, however, the large sums of £1,575,898 for the increase of the army, and nearly £2,000,000 for the navy were voted; and new taxes were imposed in order to meet this unprecedented demand

In Ireland the campaign had been decisive. The troops under Ginckel had beaten the French supporters of James, and the siege and capitulation of Limerick put an end to the attempted invasion, though the miseries which it caused long continued. Of the 14,000 or 15,000 soldiers who were allowed to march out of that city with the honours of war, about 10,000 embarked for France, entered the French army, and were afterwards famous as "the Irish Brigade." Meanwhile the fleet under the command of Russell had done nothing, and the trade of England had been almost ruined by French privateers, while numerous plots and conspiracies were detected, and important changes were made, some of which converted dismissed Whigs into vehement Jacobites.

Among those who were dismissed from all appointments was Churchill, earl of Marlborough, who was variously accused of being in communication with St. Germains, of taking bribes, and of causing divisions in the army. As his wife, the clever and fearless Sarah Jennings, had for years been the intimate friend of the Princess Anne, this event greatly increased the ill feeling which had for some time existed between the queen and her sister, and had probably been caused by the fact that Anne had also been in communication with James, with a view of keeping on the safe side in case of another restoration, which at one time seemed by no means improbable.

On the 5th of March, 1692, William set out for the grand campaign of the army of the confederacy, which was at Louvain; but though he did much to check the advance of the French arms he was unable to obtain any decisive successes. Namur was taken by the skill of the great engineer Vauban. The allies failed in their attempt to surprise Mons, and the battle of Steinkirk was lost, in consequence, it is said, of the inactivity of the Dutch general, Count Solines; though the engagement was so desperate, and the British infantry were so indomitable, that the enemy were unable to take any advantage of their alleged victory. Happily the victory of La Hogue retrieved the English prestige at sea, even in spite of the indifference of the admiral in command. Russell had sailed from the Downs in search of the French fleet, and was joined off Beachy Head by the squadrons of Carta and Delaval, who had been watching the French ports, and by a number of Dutch vessels, making in all ninety-nine men of war. On the 19th of May the French fleet of sixty-three ships, commanded by De Tourville, was discovered off Cape Barfleur, bearing down full upon the English, many of whose ships had not hove in sight. The engagement, which lasted from ten in the morning till five in the evening, was a desultory one, the combatants being too far distant from each other to make any but long shots, and then the French towed away with all their boats, with the English still in pursuit. The engagement was resumed, but a fog came on, and De Tourville, perhaps relying on the sailing qualities of his ships, made for the westward. At noon the next day when the fog had cleared there were two leagues between the fleets, but on the following morning a brisk gale had enabled a number of the French vessels to make their way into the "Race of Alderney," that narrow strait which divides the rugged island from the peninsula of Contentin, and whose saw-like jagged rocks and baffling currents make it a dangerous passage in stormy weather especially for large ships. Sir John Ashley, admiral of the blue, and the Commander of the Dutch squadron, followed with their vessels as far as the mouth of the Channel, but would not risk further pursuit, and stood off, while twenty-six of the enemy's vessels got away to St. Malo, for which Sir John afterwards was called to account by parliament and acquitted, though the nation did not so readily forgive him.

Sir Ralph Delaval, vice-admiral of the red, had kept toward Cherbourg, where he found stranded or dismasted De Tourville's ship the *Soleil Royal* of 119 guns, the *Admirable* of 102 guns, the *Conquerant* of 80 guns and three smaller vessels, and burned them all: but eighteen French ships of the line had got safely to La Hogue between forts De Lisset and De la Hogue. Russell was so long in reaching them that the French had time to run them aground and drag them into the shallows with their broadsides towards the enemy, while batteries and stages had already been raised on shore and furnished with the artillery of an army with which James was again to attempt the invasion of England. Among the shoals and on the beach were shallops filled with infantry, and above on the heights stood the army itself with James, the Duke of Berwick, Marshal de Belfonde, and other generals and officers of the staff.

The next morning (the 22d of May) they witnessed a new and terrible spectacle, for it was then that the battle of La Hogue was fought, not by Russell but by Vice-admiral Rooke, who was sent by his commander to attempt the desperate duty of advancing with the men in light frigates and in open boats into the shallow water, and thence to fight their way on board or to burn the enemy's vessels, as best they could. He stood as near as possible in the frigates, while the sailors

with undaunted valour pulled steadily towards the shore under a terrible fire of guns and musketry. There was only one way of doing the work that they had to accomplish, and they took it. Rowing close up to the stranded vessels they flung away oars and muskets, and, with their cutlasses in their hands and a loud huzza, sprang up to the decks of the French, and carrying all before them pointed the guns against the forts and the shallops. It is said that even the stupid and unheroic James was so carried away when he witnessed this exploit, that he momentarily forgot its cause and consequence, and exclaimed, "See my brave English sailors;" but when six French ships of the line were burned that night, when on the following day the rest of the fleet at La Hogue with the transports and merchant vessels were destroyed, and when as the fire reached the water's edge several of the loaded guns exploded and killed some of the persons who stood near him, he said, "Heaven fights against me," and retired hopelessly to his tent, soon to return to St. Germains, where, however, he for several years continued to make efforts to regain the crown.

QUEEN ANNE.

On the death of William III. the contest for power between Whigs and Tories was renewed with such persistency that the reign of Anne may be regarded as a period of constant political intrigue, and had it not been for the fact that England had already entered on a system of constitutional government, the country might again have been divided by civil war, for the queen was constantly under the influence of those personal favourites who had for years been able to persuade and to control her. It may indeed be said that the Duchess of Marlborough was for several years the actual sovereign, and that John Churchill, her husband, was the most exalted personage in the realm.

A consummate general, possessed of a faculty of self-control and an impenetrable reticence which almost equalled the same qualities that distinguished William himself, Marlborough had been regarded by the king, not perhaps as a rival in the art of command, but as a man who required constant and almost suspicious attention. He was too important to be neglected, especially as it was to his influence and that of his duchess that Anne had yielded when she espoused the cause of the revolution, and refrained from communicating with James at St. Germains. At the same time Marlborough's great abilities were enhanced by a remarkable courtesy and dignity of manner, which, united to a singularly fine presence and handsome person, gave him an undoubted advantage. The rise of John Churchill had been accelerated by these qualities, and from an obscure lieutenant with little learning and scarcely anything beyond his pay, he had, by his caution, his courage, and a certain natural eloquence and address, attained, while he was yet a youth, to a position which many a man of nobler principles and greater patriotism might have sought for in vain. His sister, Arabella Churchill, was one of the mistresses of James II., and to her influence he may have owed the first promotion from which he afterwards steadily advanced to the highest position of almost any subject in Europe; but it was by the extraordinary influence which his wife had gained over the Princess Anne that he was enabled to use those undoubtedly great talents as a general which eventually humbled the power of France, and made his name feared where his character could not be respected.

It is impossible to refer to the position occupied by the Duchess of Marlborough without remembering that in the terse sentences of Macaulay we find a striking description of the power which she exercised over the queen. The understanding of Anne was sluggish, and though there was latent in her character a hereditary wilfulness and stubbornness which, many years later, great power and great provocations developed, she was yet a willing slave to a nature far more vivacious and imperious than her own. This nature was found in Sarah Jennings, whose elder sister Frances had been distinguished by beauty and levity even among the crowd of beautiful faces and light characters which adorned and disgraced Whitehall during the wild carnival of the Restoration. Sarah, less regularly beautiful, was perhaps more attractive. Her face was expressive, her form wanted no feminine charm, and the profusion of her fine hair, not yet disguised by powder according to that barbarous fashion which she lived to see introduced, was the delight of numerous admirers.

Among the gallants who sued for her favour Colonel Churchill, young, handsome, graceful, insinuating, eloquent, and brave, obtained the preference. He must have been enamoured indeed; for he had little property except the annuity which he had bought with a sum of money bestowed on him by the Duchess of Cleveland, with whom he had, when a mere youth, been an accepted lover. He was insatiable of riches: Sarah was poor, and a plain girl with a large fortune was proposed to him. His love, after a struggle, prevailed over his avarice: marriage only strengthened his passion, and, to the last hour of his life, Sarah enjoyed the pleasure and distinction of being the one human being who was able to mislead that far-sighted and sure-footed judgment, who was fervently loved by that cold heart, and who was servilely feared by that intrepid spirit.

In a worldly sense the fidelity of Churchill's love was amply rewarded. His bride, though slenderly portioned, brought with her a dowry which, judiciously employed, made him at length a duke of England, a prince of the empire, the captain-general of a great coalition, the arbiter between mighty princes, and, what he valued more, the wealthiest subject in Europe. She had been brought up from childhood with the Princess Anne, and a close friendship had arisen between the girls. In character they resembled each other very little. Anne was slow and taciturn. To those whom she loved she was meek. The form which her anger assumed was sullenness. She had a strong sense of religion, and was attached even with bigotry to the rites and government of the Church of England.

Sarah was lively and voluble, domineered over those whom she regarded with most kindness, and when she was offended vented her rage in tears and tempestuous reproaches. To sanctity she made no pretence, and indeed narrowly escaped the imputation of irreligion. She was not yet what she became when one class of vices had been fully developed in her by prosperity and another by adversity, when her brain had been turned by success and flattery, when her heart had been ulcerated by disasters and mortifications. She lived to be that most odious and miserable of human beings an ancient crone, at war with her whole kind, at war with her own children and grand-children, valuing greatness and riches chiefly because they enabled her to brave public opinion, and to indulge without restraint her hatred to the living and the dead. Yet this woman had for years been loved and even worshipped by Anne. Prince George, a dull man whose chief pleasures were derived from his dinners and his bottle, gave himself up with stupid patience to the dominion of the vehement and commanding spirit by which his wife was governed. Anne had several children, none of whom survived infancy, and she had for them a true maternal tenderness; but her love for them was languid when compared with her devotion to the companion of her early years. The titles which etiquette prescribed were distasteful to her when used by her friend. Anne was Mrs. Morley, Lady Churchill was Mrs. Freeman, and under these childish names was carried on during twenty years a correspondence on which at last the fate of administrations and dynasties depended.

The queen began her reign with a prepossession for the Tories; in the words of her favourite, the Duchess of Marlborough, she "had from her infancy imbibed the most unconquerable prejudice against the Whigs. She had been taught to look upon them all, not only as republicans who hated the very shadow of regal authority, but as implacable enemies to the Church of England. This aversion to the whole party had been confirmed by the ill usage she had met with from her sister and King William, which, though perhaps more owing to Lord Rochester than to any man then living, was now to be all charged to the account of the Whigs. And Prince George, her husband, who had also been ill treated in that reign, threw into the scale his resentment. On the other hand, the Tories had the advantage not only of the queen's early prepossessions in their favour, but of their having assisted her in the late reign in the affair of her settlement. It was indeed evident that they had done this more in opposition to King William than from any real respect for the Princess of Denmark. But still they had served her. And the winter before she came to the crown, they had, in the same spirit of opposition to the king and in prospect of his death, paid her more than usual civilities and attendance. It is no great wonder therefore, all these things considered, that as soon as she was seated on the throne the Tories (whom she usually called by the name of the church party) became the distinguished objects of the royal favour; and I am firmly persuaded that notwithstanding her majesty's extraordinary affection for me, and the entire devotion which my Lord Marlborough and my Lord Godolphin had for many years showed to her service, they would not have had so great a share of her favour and confidence if they had not been reckoned of the Tories."

That the Tories were in power there can be no doubt, and Rochester, who would have restored a test act and the persecution of Dissenters, was an upholder of hereditary right and non-resistance, which her grace of Marlborough characterizes as "gibberish," which she could not think to forebode good to her mistress, whose title rested upon a different foundation. Indeed Marlborough and Godolphin were not really such high Tories as to follow men like Rochester, or even St. John, who, having been a Nonconformist, became the advocate of intolerance in order to attain to favour; but Marlborough also joined those who advocated the revival of penal statutes against Dissenters, though he afterwards trimmed his sails in conformity with the mixed Whig and Tory government, of which St. John was secretary at war, and Harley chief secretary of state.

By that time Marlborough was approaching the height of his fame, the hero of Blenheim, the great general whose name alone caused terror among the enemy. Yet this great man, whose military ability and genius for command had given to England the foremost place in Europe, who had been rewarded with truly royal munificence, and whose palace of Blenheim House was a more than royal residence, was to lose his influence by the intrigues of St. John (Bolingbroke) and Harley, who contrived to make of a poor cousin of the Duchess of Marlborough a rival to that powerful favourite of the queen.

The Tory government had been succeeded by one entirely under the control of the Whigs, who were the allies of Marlborough and his duchess, and the only hope of the aspirants to power was to find some means of diminishing their influence over the queen, who had perhaps herself become sensible of the kind of thraldom in which she had long been held by her now rather arrogant and exacting friend. The two unscrupulous ministers found an instrument for supplanting the duchess in Mistress Abigal Hill, a cousin of her own and also a relation of Mr. Harley. The favourite had introduced this lady to court as a bedchamber woman to the queen. In the summer of 1707 the duchess learned that this, her protegée, was privately married to a Mr. Masham, that the queen had been present at the wedding, which took place at Dr. Arbuthnot's lodgings, and that her majesty had already made her "an absolute favourite," with the privileges which the duchess alone had so long enjoyed of private and confidential relations.

This was the beginning of that long series of plots and counterplots, which, although they were themselves often contemptible, and were promoted by unscrupulous and treacherous men, were followed by the most important events in English history. Bolingbroke and his ally Mrs. Masham were in constant communication with St. Germains, and desired the succession to the throne to be settled on the Pretender instead of on the Elector of Hanover; but Marlborough, who had left England shorn of all his offices though not of his enormous wealth, was still a powerful and influential foe, calmly awaiting at Ostend the death of Anne who had first raised him to the highest pitch of authority and then debased him, and looking forward to the resumption of his place in the House of Peers and his great command in the army under the favour of George I., the energy and promptitude of the Whigs having overcome all the preparations made for an attempt to proclaim the son of Marie d'Este.

It is only by remembering that the government of the country had been settled as a constitution, that we can at all appreciate the enormous importance of the events which took place under the rule of a sovereign like Anne; though her combined timidity and obstinacy actually tended to determine both the form of the constitution itself and the occurrences which influenced the position of the great nations of Europe. While the contention of parties was supported by ignoble artifices, it led to extraordinary results, and though the queen was so weak as to have constantly been swayed by the imperious demands of her favourite, that favourite was herself so imperious that her demands enabled the party of which her husband was a member to concede to him the power which for a time, aided by his calm, determined, and intrepid temper, broke the influence of France, and by a great coalition of which he was the acknowledged head, achieved that which William III. might have failed to accomplish.

It is interesting after reading of the splendid triumphs of Marlborough to turn first to those letters which passed between "Mrs. Morley and Mrs. Freeman," and then to the account of the commonplace quarrel in which Anne obstinately refused either to answer or to listen to the reproaches of her intimate friend before banishing her from her councils, and depriving her husband of those great offices which had been the reward of such vast national successes. At the same time these very characteristics of combined weakness and obstinacy often had the curious effect of frustrating the attempts of either party to attain permanent authority. Swift says: "The queen grew so jealous upon the change of her servants, that often, from the fear of being imposed on and over caution, she would impose upon herself. She took a delight in refusing those who were thought to have had the greatest power with her even in the most reasonable things, nor would she let them be done until she fell into the humour of it herself." This, which may be regarded as an infirmity of temper, contributed no little to the balance of parties which, at the time of her death, left the Whigs in power, and had frequently before baffled the tactics of men who, while they represented some of her own most cherished convictions, were themselves only seeking to obtain the rewards of place or the gratification of ambition.

It would seem indeed as though the stupendous events of this reign turned on pivots so insignificant, that we can scarcely regard them alone without a kind of scornful surprise. And yet the personal character of Anne was far from being contemptible: her presence was royal, her manners gracious, and her person comely and distinguished by a plain but most attractive dignity. She was spoken of and remembered as "good Queen Anne," and not without reason, for she had little if any of the arbitrary selfishness of her race, and displayed a genuine affection for her subjects and a desire to promote their happiness. She was also capable of a wide generosity and of a royal munificence in dispensing her charities. Of this, her again devoting to the church the "first-fruits" and other emoluments which had been seized by the crown was only an example; though the poor clergy, to increase whose incomes that large fund was transferred, fitly commemorated it under the name of Queen Anne's bounty

It must be remembered too, that the revival of literature following the better establishment of government distinguished this period of English history. We may hesitate to call it "the Augustan age" of letters, except in the sense that it was a time when a great number of men distinguished for ability wrote on almost every conceivable subject. Swift, Steele, Addison, Prior, Pope, and a whole galaxy of eminent names are associated with it; but it could not be truly denominated as the greatest literary period of England, for the quality of the literature falls short of that which appeared in the time of Elizabeth. Still, amidst a vast profusion of books and pamphlets, of which poems and essays form a considerable part, there are many which take their place in the national literature and cannot be forgotten.

More influential still in forming the manners and in controlling the opinions, even if it added to the fierce argumentative conflicts of the time, was that periodical literature which may be said to have sprung suddenly into existence at that period. There had been a newspaper in the reign of Elizabeth, a mere brief chronicle of government measures; there were pamphlets and newsletters during the troublous times of Charles I., and they increased in number, in importance, and in virulence after the restoration of the Stuarts; but it was during the reign of Anne that the newspaper and the weekly periodical became recognized powers in the direction of public intelligence, and were regularly read not only by the frequenters of the coffee-houses who regularly assembled to discuss public affairs and private scandals, but by quiet country gentlemen who had their magazines from town, and by citizens and tradesmen who looked to them for information if not for instruction.

The domestic virtue of the queen, and the consequent morality of the court as compared with those of Charles and James, effected a vast social improvement, while the union of England and Scotland, although it gave little satisfaction at the time, was an event which tended greatly to consolidate the national sentiment, and to preserve the kingdom from subsequent attempts to re-establish the claims both of the first and the second Pretender.

GEORGE THE FIRST.

The jealousy exhibited by Anne at the proposal for George, the Electoral Prince of Hanover, to come over to England seemed at one time to favour the revival of plots to bring in the Pretender. Schemes and intrigues in his favour were of almost daily occurrence, and the Duke of Berwick urged that he should go privately and alone to

England, should present himself to his sister, and persuade her to go down to parliament and there represent that his right to the crown was incontestable; that she had resolved to restore him to his right, and had taken measures to prevent any danger to the Church of England, it having been settled that during her life he was to be educated in England as her heir and successor.

The Whigs were alarmed, but they were vigilant, and the movements of the Pretender were closely watched and reported both to them and to the court of Hanover. The Jacobites, aided by Mrs. Masham, had determined on the fall of Oxford and the restoration of Bolingbroke, who, indifferent as he was to religion, upheld the High Church party, and succeeded in promoting the renewal of oppressive measures against Nonconformists. On the other hand, there were a large number of Tories, who, though they were but cold and unsympathetic allies of the Whigs, and were violent High Churchmen, preferred the accession of the Guelphs to the restoration of the Stuarts. It was understood too that Marlborough, who had sent money to the court at St. Germains, was yet ready to uphold the Hanoverian claims, and had also offered to send £20,000 to enable Prince George to come over to England. This self-contained and sagacious speculator was waiting at Ostend watching events, and ready to return when he should hear of the death of Anne, that he might throw the weight of his power and influence into whichever scale best suited his purpose.

The queen was dying. Agitated by the quarrels of the court and the stormy debates in parliament, undecided, and yet governed by those personal feelings which at one time yielded to private favouritism and at another left her obstinately determined to assert her own right, she was stricken down by apoplexy, and afterwards fell into a stupor from which she never recovered. The nation grieved for her, but at the same time the great majority of thoughtful men foresaw that if her life were prolonged, and arbitrary power remained in the hands of the unscrupulous and intriguing ministry to which she had committed herself, the liberties of the country would be in peril.

That power they had not yet grasped. Bolingbroke, Ormond, Harcourt, and their supporters, were nominated to offices of which they had not yet taken possession. They therefore summoned a hasty council at Kensington, not far from where the queen lay insensible. Before anything could be discussed the Dukes of Argyle and Somerset arrived and took their seats at the council-board, saying, that hearing of the queen's danger they had hastened to offer their services. Bolingbroke saw that the Whigs had been too prompt for him. The Duke of Shrewsbury, who was present, rose to thank the new comers for their prompt assistance, and they, after having sent for and examined the physicians, declared that the post of lord-treasurer should at once be filled, and insisted on going at once to her majesty to recommend her to appoint Shrewsbury to the office.

Argyle had marched troops to London; seven battalions were on their way from Dunkirk. Means were taken to equip a fleet by an embargo on all the seaports. General Stanhope, Marlborough's son-in-law, had taken steps to quell any Jacobite rising, and so all attempts to bring in the Pretender were rendered futile. The council went at once to the queen's bedside accompanied by Bolingbroke, who saw that his power was gone. Whether Anne understood the questions addressed to her may be doubtful, but a nod or a gesture was interpreted to mean assent, and Lord Shrewsbury, already lord-chamberlain and Lord-lieutenant of Ireland, was made lord-treasurer and prime minister, and the accession of the House of Hanover was decided. The heralds and a troop of life-guards were held in readiness to proclaim the new king directly after the death of the queen; and Mr. Secretary Craggs was sent off to Hanover to hasten the journey of the elector, who was to join the English fleet on the coast of Holland.

On the following morning, the 31st July, 1714, Anne died in the fiftieth year of her age, and the Elector of Hanover was proclaimed with acclamation in London and the principal cities. On the next evening Marlborough reached Dover, and thence made a sort of triumphal progress to the metropolis. Parliament met on the day of the queen's death (Sunday), and again the next day. A civil list was passed for £700,000, and a reward of £100,000 was offered for the apprehension of the Pretender in case of his landing on these shores.

George I. was in no hurry to take possession of the throne. His stolidity almost appeared to amount to indifference, and his plain appearance and dull manner were not calculated to remove the impression. It was not till the 18th of September, seven weeks after the death of Anne, that he landed at Greenwich with his eldest son, Prince George; but the Hanoverians had witnessed his departure with regret, and his new subjects received him with no small show of welcome. On the

20th of October the coronation was performed at Westminster Abbey with all the usual solemnities.

The whole disposition of the great offices of state was now on the Whig side. Manifestos were issued condemning the assumptions of the House of Stuart, and the most prominent Tories of the late ministry were impeached, many of them being arrested, and Oxford sent to the Tower, whither he was soon followed by the famous Matthew Prior, the secretary, who steadfastly refused to betray any of his master's secrets, or to give evidence against him. Lord Halifax was made chancellor of the exchequer; Lord Cowper was lord-chancellor; Marlborough, commander-in-chief; Nottingham, president of the council; Oxford, first lord of the admiralty; Shrewsbury, lord-chamberlain; Walpole, the brilliant debater, was paymaster of the forces, an appointment of great value, and in Scotland the Jacobite Earl of Mar was replaced by the Duke of Montrose, while Argyle was intrusted with the command of the forces.

Very soon, however, the attempts of the supporters of the Pretender were renewed and civil war again raged in Scotland, where Mar had raised the standard of the Stuarts in the Highlands, whence, not having either the ability of a Montrose or a Dundee, he made ineffectual attempts, which were frustrated, but only by prolonged suffering and bloodshed. The Duke of Ormond, the Duke of Berwick, and Bolingbroke, who had escaped to France, were assiduous among the Jacobites at the French court to obtain assistance for the insurgents; but Louis XIV. was dead, and the dissolute regent, Orleans, could not be persuaded that James Francis Edward had any great chance of success either in Scotland or England. A time had arrived when France and England were in co-operation against Spain. The "triple alliance" of England, France, and Holland, and the "quadruple" alliance which followed, and included the House of Austria, eventually gave a twelve years' peace to Europe.

THE ESCAPE OF LORD NITHSDALE FROM THE TOWER.

The ill-ordered insurrection commenced by the Earl of Mar, for the restoration of the Pretender, may be said to have ended in the battle of Sheriffmuir; that fierce engagement, in which the Highlanders fought so fiercely and sternly, that though the victory remained with Argyle and Wightman, the insurgent chief also took with him trophies of the contested field when he retired to Perth, leaving his opponents unable to follow up their advantage. After that the attempts to place James Francis Edward Stuart on the English throne were merely desultory failures, often without earnestness, except among a few misguided men who succumbed not only to the power of established government, or to the treachery of their former adherents, but also to the weakness and vacillation of the puny prince for whom so many brave lives were sacrificed, and so much misery and suffering endured.

The engagement, which ended in the loss of 700 killed and 200 prisoners by the insurgents, and 400 killed and 200 prisoners by the royal army, was represented in France as a success, or at all events was concealed as a defeat; and though the Regent Orleans could not be induced to believe in the ultimate success of the partisans of the Stuart cause, perhaps an undoubted victory on the side of the rebels might have induced him to send them substantial aid, but all that he did was to refrain from preventing "the Chevalier" from leaving France, however he may have feigned to intercept him. Indeed, it is probable that he would have been glad to get rid of so troublesome a guest.

The prince had left Lorraine for the coast before he heard the true version of the battle of Sheriffmuir; and as the Jacobites in Scotland were entreating him to come, as Mar declared that he was stronger since the engagement with Argyle, and that he had 16,000 fighting men under his command, and as Bolingbroke and Berwick both urged him to embark at once, he set out in a small vessel from Dunkirk, with six gentlemen, who, like himself, were disguised as naval officers, and arrived at Peterhead on the 22d of December, 1715. Hence he went, still disguised, through Aberdeen to Fetteresso, where he was joined by Lord Mar, General Hamilton, and about thirty others who had hastened across the country, leaving the army behind them. If the Pretender had no royal qualification he seems to have delighted in playing at prerogative, for he stayed for some days at Fetteresso, keeping a sort of court, receiving compliments and professions of loyalty, and dispensing favours and titles, among which was a dukedom which he bestowed on Mar. There were shrewd suspicions that he was afraid to go forward lest he should encounter Argyle, and that his inactivity had less to do with the ague from which he was said to be suffering, than with his uncertainty of the number and locality of the king's troops. In about ten days he removed to Kinnaird, and thence to Glammis Castle, the ancient and magnificent seat of the Earl of Strathmore. On the 6th of January he entered Dundee with Mar and the earl-marshal riding one on each side of him, and attended by 300 Jacobite lords and gentlemen. In the market-place he halted for an hour while people thronged to kiss his hand, and then went forward to the royal palace of Scone, which is near Perth, where the insurgent army had taken up its quarters. Thence he issued manifestos and proclamations, but he failed to make a favourable impression, for he was both weak and self-willed. Perhaps he had inherited a disposition to equivocate and to make false representations, a characteristic that his education by the Jesuits had developed, and while he exhibited the obstinacy and the talent for subterfuge which seemed to belong to his family he was personally timid and irresolute.

There was much to disappoint and to depress him. Instead of the 16,000 men promised by Mar there were not more than 6000, and several of the influential Highland chiefs had seceded from the cause and made terms with the government, carrying with them their clansmen, who were ready to fight for any party which their leaders favoured. This was notably the case with the infamous Simon Lord Lovat, that crafty old fox, who was later caught in the toils and ended a life of treachery on the scaffold. He had made terms with Sutherland, and marched off with his Highlanders to defeat Mackenzie at Inverness, while the rest of the Frasers, when they heard that the chief had abandoned the Stuart cause, threw away their white cockades and joined the royal army.

The dejection of the Pretender was soon shared by his adherents.

One of them said, "We found ourselves not at all animated by his presence, and if he was disappointed in us we were tenfold more so in him. We saw nothing in him that looked like spirit. He never appeared with cheerfulness and vigour to animate us. Our men began to despise him. Some asked if he could speak."

Meantime Argyle was active, and the royal troops were well supplied with money, arms, and provisions. On the 16th of January the prince held a council at Perth, at which he said it would be no new thing for him to be unfortunate. His whole life from his cradle had been a constant series of misfortunes, and he was prepared, if it so pleased God, to suffer the threats of his enemies and the enemies of his supporters. It was resolved to impede the advance of Argyle by burning and destroying all the towns and villages between Perth and Stirling, with the corn, forage, and supplies that might be found in them. A proclamation to this effect was signed by the Pretender, and the horrible determination was carried out. The blackened ruins of huts and homesteads smoked in the wintry air. The men who could bear arms were already in one or other of the opposing armies; the poor women and children, the aged and the infirm, were left homeless and destitute, exposed to the rigours of one of the most inclement winters that had been known for many years, and numbers of them perished with cold and hunger.

The Duke of Argyle and General Cadogan advanced with soldiers and peasants, clearing the roads as they went, for the snow lay deep and the drifts stood high. In spite of interruption by skirmishing parties of Highlanders from a few small garrisons on the borders of Fife, the royal troops made such progress that they advanced to join a detachment which had gone forward and driven the Highlanders out of Tullibardine.

This was but eight miles from Perth, and the court there was in confusion and dismay. On the 30th of January, the anniversary of the execution of Charles I., the Pretender prepared for flight, and on the following day, when Argyle was advancing, the town was fast emptying, the prince and his army defiling across the broad stream of the Tay, which was then so frozen as to allow both horse and foot to pass. Mar and the Pretender pushed on along the Carse of Gowrie to Dundee; but Argyle followed, though more slowly, and found that town also deserted.

The light-footed and hardy Highlanders had struck along the road to Montrose, on a way so deep with snow that Cadogan followed by another route, and only reached Arbroath on the 5th of February, to learn that the Pretender had fled to France. He had ordered the faithful clans to be ready to march with him at night to Aberdeen, where he said they would find a considerable force from the Continent. At the appointed time horses were ready at the door of the house in which he was lodged, and a guard of honour awaited him, but he had escaped by the back-door, had gone to Lord Mar's quarters, and thence by a by-way to the water side, where a boat was waiting to carry him and some of his followers to the *Maria Therese*, a French ship from St. Malo. Mar accompanied him, and two other boats took on board the Earl of Melfort, Lord Drummond, Lieutenant-general Sheldon, and ten other gentlemen. The vessel put to sea immediately, and thus this miserable enterprise ended in the cowardly and cunning flight of the prince in whose cause so many brave men had lost their fortunes and their lives. He left the money he had with him, with a letter to Argyle, asking him to use it for relieving the sufferings of the poor people whose villages had been burned; and to General Gordon he sent a letter, saying, that the disappointments he had met with, especially from abroad, had compelled him to leave the country, and advising them to seek their own safety as best they might.

The Highland army sought the glens and mountain passes, where it melted away as it went, amidst the rude homes of those who had so lately fought in its ranks. But thousands of Englishmen and Scots had afterwards to pay the penalty. The royal troops were placed at free quarters in the houses and on the estates of the Jacobites, and though the numbers of prisoners in the Highlands was small, the clans were let loose upon each other. In the north of England, however, the jails were full. High Church divines, Popish priests and monks in disguise, gentlemen squires, officers, Highland chiefs, Lowland lairds, and numbers of the common people, were taken. Many were executed by military law, numbers were left to starve and perish of cold and privation in castles and jails. The most conspicuous of the leaders were marched to London, and after crossing Finchley Common, were made to halt on the brow of Highgate Hill, whence they were taken with hands bound behind their backs, their horses led by foot-soldiers, amidst the beating of drums, and the scoffs, shouts, and insults of the multitude. The lords and noblemen were sent to the Tower, the rest to the common jails. Among the former were James, earl of Derwentwater, Lord Widdrington, the Earls of Nithsdale, Winton, and Carnwath, Viscount Kenmure, and Lord Nairn.

Lord Winton pleaded not guilty, and was reserved for a trial, which did not take place till three months afterwards, when he was found guilty, but not executed; he was committed to the Tower, whence he contrived to escape. The rest threw themselves on the mercy of the crown, and great efforts were made on behalf of two of them: the Earl of Derwentwater and Lord Nairn. The life of the latter was saved by the interposition of his old schoolfellow, Secretary Stanhope; but nothing could save Derwentwater, though his lovely countess and many ladies of high rank strove to move the king to mercy. George was not naturally cruel or implacable, but he was dull, and regarded the crime as one in regard to which he must follow the advice of his ministers. Bribes were offered in vain, £60,000 being promised for Derwentwater's life; but though many of the Whigs were inclined to be lenient, Walpole and some others would not listen to any favour for "rebels and parricides." Some favourable circumstances were discovered for Carnwath and Widdrington, and they were respited.

The three remaining victims therefore were Derwentwater, Kenmure, and Nithsdale. For the former many honest hearts grieved, and on every hillside and in every valley in Cumberland tears were shed for his misfortune. Execution was to follow quickly after sentence, and a message was sent to the Tower to have the block ready the following morning. Yet the courage and devotion of a woman robbed the headsman of one of the three; Lady Nithsdale had been permitted to bid her husband farewell, and she seized the opportunity to prevail on him to dress himself in female attire and so to escape from prison that very night.[1] The Countess of Derwentwater was less fortunate, and her lord, with Kenmure, were led to the scaffold on the following morning.

---

[1] The treatment of the subject by the artist was suggested by the following extract from a letter written by the Countess of Nithsdale, to her sister the Lady Mary Herbert. "I had taken care," she says, "that Mrs. Mills did not go out crying as she had come in, that my lord might the better pass for the lady who came in crying and afflicted, and the more so because he had on the same dress she wore. . . . I went out leading him by the hand, and he held his handkerchief to his eyes. . . . The guards opened the doors, and I went down stairs with him, still conjuring him to make all possible despatch."

GEORGE THE SECOND.

The dislike to George I. which Jacobite conspirators endeavoured to increase, by continually publishing accounts of his dull and heavy appearance, his coarseness, and the ugliness and rapacity of his mistresses, had some effect, inasmuch as a great deal of what was said was true; and yet there was so much of honesty of purpose and of blunt determination about the man, that the people of England could not consent to exchange him for the feeble prince who had so signally failed in provoking a revolution, and was both a debauchee and a Papist. George, who was the representative of that branch of the Guelph family which sprung from the marriage of Henry the Lion with Matilda, daughter of Henry II. of England, had been intended as the husband of Anne, but married instead, his cousin, Sophia Dorothea of Zell. The match was the result of family policy, and probably was against the inclination of the princess, whose alleged intrigue with Count Philip von Konigsmarck was discovered by the elector Ernest Augustus, the father of George, during the absence of the latter from Hanover; an event which led to the assassination of Konigsmarck, the imprisonment of Sophia Dorothea, and probably the determination of George to keep his queen out of England, which she never visited, though she lived to within a few months of the death of her husband. It is believed that the persistency of George, Prince of Wales, in defending the reputation of his mother, was one of the causes of the bitter animosity which for some time existed between him and his father. This animosity resulted in quarrels, which were only superficially made up some time before the death of the king, which happened unexpectedly on a journey to Osnabrück, during which he was seized with an apoplectic fit and died in his carriage.

Marlborough was dead, and while he lay on his death-bed the Jacobite conspiracies revived. The Pretender had married the Princess Clementina, grand-daughter of the heroic John Sobieski, King of Poland; and at the end of the year 1720 she had given birth to a son, at whose birth seven cardinals, appointed for the purpose by the Pope, were in attendance, and who received the name of Charles Edward

Louis Casimir. The usual schemes were adopted by the Jacobites in all parts of the kingdom. Comparisons were drawn between the Stuarts and the Guelphs. Scurrilous lampoons were directed against the king and his ugly and rapacious mistresses; and while such means were taken to influence the masses, deeper plotters were actually preparing for a revolution. The perspicacity and prompt energy of Walpole frustrated these intentions, however, and the nation was saved from what would have been a determined and widely organized plot. It was with more difficulty that the astute minister contrived to sustain the injured credit of the country, which had become the prey of bubble companies, of which the South Sea Scheme was the most fatal to those who were concerned in it. The collapse of this gigantic association, which had been sustained by a system of remarkable frauds on capitalists and on the public, affected the financial stability, not only of English commercial enterprise, but of the principal states in Europe; and many eminent persons in this country were either tried as accomplices in the nefarious transactions of the company, or were obliged to retire to the Continent, ruined in fortune if not in reputation.

England was only just recovering from the effects of a series of the wildest schemes for making money by absurd pretences, when George Augustus succeeded to the throne. As Prince of Wales he had long been the centre of a kind of opposition court, and his popularity, such as it was, had doubtless added to the inimical feelings with which his father regarded him, and to the unseemly and bitter, though trivial, quarrels which were only at last (in 1720) brought to an end, as far as outward demonstrations were concerned, by the intermediation of friends of both parties. Of the character and ability of George II. it is difficult to speak, since those who were supposed to be most intimate with him, and who have left some biographical sketches, speak of him with an almost virulent sarcasm, which leaves in the mind of the reader a feeling of mingled aversion and distrust. Horace Walpole, Lord Chesterfield, and Lord Hervey, should each have had ample opportunities of describing the king in his habit as he lived, but each in his way was prejudiced and unscrupulous, Walpole in his relish for a racy story apart from its truth; Chesterfield as the renegade who occupied the same position in the household of Frederick, the succeeding Prince of Wales, as he had formerly maintained in that of George Augustus; and Herbert as a man not only unscrupulous but unabashed

even by personal association with occurrences which he marks as infamous in others.

It would seem that the indications of character in George II. must be judged partly from his peculiarity of temperament. He was at once weaker and more generally accomplished than his father, more affable and less true, with a wider range of thought and observation, but less self-contained and thorough in his convictions as to the duties and the claims of his position. Little accidents or untoward events disturbed him so much that he ceased to be master even of his outward aspect and manner. In private he was parsimonious and even mean, but he was always ready to spend money freely in the public service. He had in fact very little notion of being a king except in a public capacity, and this may be a fault or a virtue according to the point of view from which it is regarded. During his reign the national debt was very nearly doubled, and yet he had the reputation of being stingy, and his mode of living was frugal in the extreme. At the same time his foreign policy was daring, and it required all the tact of Walpole to control it within moderate bounds, especially as George Augustus had as much regard to the welfare of Hanover as had been displayed by his father, and would often have made the interest of England subservient to that of the principality. This desire to initiate a foreign policy found an ally in the elder Pitt, who succeeded Walpole, and may have been allied to the physical courage which made the battlefield a fitting arena for the impetuous and courageous little monarch who had about him something of the heroic, which contrasted in a very marked manner with the unobtrusive resolution of George I. Another peculiarity of his was that he never scrupled to talk about his own bravery, so that persons not acquainted with his real character were ready to doubt its reality, especially as his vanity occasionally found outward expression in a strutting gait and a stage attitude, which gave the wild wits of the time a theme for their most audacious lampoons. It is declared by astute observers that he thus demonstratively laid claim to a qualification that he really possessed, because, in spite of a certain arrogance, he really distrusted himself in matters of state-craft, and knew that though he could thoroughly appreciate an able policy, he had not sufficient ability to inaugurate one.

He was at once exacting and extreme in his attachments and vehement in his antipathies. He had a sincere affection for his wife, though he treated her with the same disregard to her feelings as he did most people with whom he was intimate. He displayed a queer kind of maundering sentimentality, which led him to be a voluminous letter-writer, describing, either to his wife or to his mistress, all his thoughts, hopes, fears, and vague imaginations; and he would talk in the same fashion either in his wife's apartments, or while wandering about in the moonlight with an actual mistress, with the Countess of Suffolk— with whom it has been supposed that he had no worse relations than this kind of dreary flirtation,—or with Madame de Valmoden, his later mistress, who after the queen's death became Countess of Yarmouth. With all his infidelity, however, George always consulted his wife about state affairs, and usually took her advice, which seems to have been that of a sound and practical mind, though she was probably influenced by Walpole. It is certain, however, that Caroline was a remarkably clear-headed, self-possessed, and managing woman, who exercised so great an influence on her husband, that he is said to have confided to her even those real or sentimental relations which would have aroused the bitter jealousy and animosity of most women. It is remarkable, too, that while knowing and caring nothing for art, and little for learning, he was most anxious to establish a reputation for the quality of bravery, of which no one could justly deny his possession; the queen desired above all things to attain to the fame of a highly intellectual person, to whom art, science, literature, philosophy, politics, and theology were familiar subjects. It would appear that neither the king nor the queen had any definite belief on the subject of religion, that is to say they were Theists, not professing any particular creed, and occupying the position of those who have generally been known as "free-thinkers."

If George II. had, when Prince of Wales, been a source of disquiet to his father, his own son Frederick was a still greater trouble both to him and to the queen. It is not to be wondered at, that this should have been so, for whether from the deficiencies of his early training, the want of restraining influences in his youth, either of religion or of example, or from a character at once weak and easily depraved, he was so thoroughly vicious that, except by a few showy and comparatively worthless accomplishments, he attracted little respect, and could not obtain the regards even of those who were his professed friends and attendants. His mother half-pitied and excused him, but could scarcely help disliking him for his folly, cowardice, meanness, and purposeless prevarication. His father seems to have despised and detested him. His death was a shock only to those who had gathered about him in order to make him, as heir apparent, the centre of a cabal, but it was little less than a relief to the nation who had looked with reluctance to his probable succession to the throne.

ENGLISH PUBLIC LOTTERIES.

So strongly has the legislature set its face of late years against the recognition of anything approaching public gambling, that in some quarters it has been twitted with having become quite "grandmotherly" in its solicitude for the morals of the people; and there is no doubt that some inconvenience, not to say oppression, has at times resulted from the laws which prohibit almost the simplest game of chance beyond the privacy of what is considered to be an Englishman's "castle," that is, the house in which he lives. But the legislation of the last half century in this respect has surely been in the right direction, even if it be admitted that it has gone to extremes; and no right thinking person can fail to admit that the statute which did away with the licensed moral evil of state lotteries was a wise and judicious measure. It at any rate put an end, in one direction, to an unwholesome craving after gain, a feverishness of mind which could not but have an ill effect upon public morals, greater even than appeared upon the surface, though that was bad enough. The wonder is, not that lotteries should have been abolished by the law, but that such sources of corruption should have been allowed to grow up under the fostering care of the state, and have had an existence down to a period within the memory of men and women now living.

State lotteries did not originate in this country, and if antiquity alone could make anything respectable, they assuredly might have claimed a patent for that quality. The Romans appear to have had their lotteries as a means of enlivening the carnivals; and coming down to a period of about three centuries ago, we find them in favour in Italy,

Germany, and elsewhere. They then passed on to France, and ultimately to England, and in the time of Elizabeth, and for long years subsequently, they were a common mode of raising money for state uses. The repair of harbours and other public works was the purpose for which the first lottery in England, in the year 1569, was put; and so convenient a mode of raising capital was not lost sight of when additions to the public revenue were required for a variety of purposes.

A document is extant which describes this first state gambling of Elizabeth as "a very rich lottery-general of money, plate, and certain sorts of merchandise erected by her majesty's order." This bait was presented to the public in the form of a large bill, bearing a representation of the royal arms, the city of London, St. Paul's Cathedral, &c.; whilst the articles which the eager drawers of the lottery were tempted to possess themselves of, such as plate, tapestry, money, &c., were also pictorially drawn out upon the placard. There were 400,000 "lots," and the price was 10s. each. The drawing began on the 11th of January, 1568-69, in a building erected by the western door of St. Paul's Cathedral, and continued till the 6th of May, the lord-mayor and the corporation of the city of London, in conjunction with the queen, standing sponsors for the genuineness of the transaction;—not only so, but the civic dignitaries themselves, as well as the guilds of the city and several of the small hamlets and parishes round London, were amongst the adventurers, the corporation taking a thousand lots. Each person adventured what he or she pleased, and the lots were divided into halves, quarters, or smaller portions. The prizes were shown at the house of Dericke, the queen's goldsmith, in Cheapside. The greatest prize was estimated at £5000, of which £3000 was to be paid in ready money, and "seven hundred poundes in plate gilte and white, and the rest in good tapissarie meet for hangings, and other covertures, and certain sortes of good linen clothe." The second prize was £3500, the third £3000, the fourth £2000, and so on down to very small sums. There were no blanks, and about 350,000 prizes were not of greater value than 2s. 6d. each.

Shortly afterwards there was a lottery for "marvellous rich and beautiful armour," the drawing or "reading" of which occupied three days, at the same place. James I. granted a lottery to be held, also at the west end of St. Paul's, "in special favour for the plantation of the English colonies in Virginia;" and one Thomas Sharplys, a tailor of

London, had the chief prize, which was plate of the value of "4000 crowns." Charles I. proposed to bring water to London by means of a lottery, and in Cromwell's time one was held in Grocers' Hall by the committee of lands for Ireland. After the Restoration people were induced by designing speculators to risk their money in lotteries for the ostensible purpose of aiding those who had suffered in the civil wars for their loyalty. From that time forward schemes were drawn up of various kinds, and the baits were held out to the public in the most alluring forms, hand-bills and placards being distributed throughout the country by tens of thousands. The halls of the city mercers, coopers, and other companies of the city of London, were used for the lotteries, as well as the Guild-hall, commissioners being appointed to superintend the drawings, which were performed by two boys, generally blue-coat boys, one being at each wheel. Insurance offices were established for the protection of speculators, and the aid of fortune-tellers was frequently invoked by eager gamblers in order to ascertain what the lucky numbers were.

A writer in the *Spectator* records how one man risked his money upon the number 1711, because that was the date of the current year; another, a great enemy to Popery, who believed that bad men were the most fortunate in this world, lay two to one on the number 666, because that was the number of the beast! A man would select the age of his wife or of a friend as his number, whilst another would take a figure which, his mind being full of lotteries, he had dreamed of. Of the hundreds of whimsical notions which possessed the minds of the adventurers one was that of a tradesman who bought four tickets, but thinking it unfortunate to have consecutive numbers, he took one back which ultimately turned up a prize of the value of £20,000! Up to the present day a farce is occasionally performed which whimsically represents the chances, and changes, and flatterings of speculators in lottery tickets. Of course the schemes were ridiculed by wits and satirists.

In Timbs's *Romance of London* it is recorded that a pamphlet was published about the year 1731, purporting to be a prospectus (by the way, that word calls up reflections on modern lotteries with a different name!) of a lottery for ladies, by which they were to obtain, as chief prize, a husband and coach and six, for £5. In 1736, an act was passed for building a bridge at Westminster by lottery, consisting of 125,000 tickets at £5 each; and the scheme was so far successful that parliament sanctioned others in succession until Westminster Bridge was completed. In 1753 the sum of £300,000 was raised by lottery for the purchase of the collections for the commencement of the British Museum; and some twenty years later the Brothers Adam, builders of the Adelphi Terrace and surrounding streets in the Strand, disposed of these and other premises in a lottery containing 110 prizes, the first drawn ticket entitling the holder to a prize of the value of £5000, and the last to one of £25,000. The work above quoted also states that one particular year was marked by a singular incident. A lottery ticket was appropriated to a child unborn, and was drawn a prize of £1000 the day after its birth. In 1767 a lady residing in Holborn had a lottery ticket presented to her by her husband, and on the Sunday preceding the drawing her success was prayed for in this form:—"The prayers of this congregation are desired for the success of a person engaged in a new undertaking."

It was not alone in London, however, that the effects of lotteries were felt. They penetrated into every part of the country, and when a prize was gained by a dweller in a remote district the excitement spread until most of the inhabitants were affected by it, and many an orgy and demoralizing scene was the consequence. Sometimes when a lucky number was announced, or when the prize was taken down by coach in charge of the agent, flags were displayed and a band was set playing, and as much fuss as possible would be made, in order to tempt other people to invest in like manner.

Lotteries existed until 1826, when the last one under the auspices of the state was drawn in Coopers' Hall, Basinghall Street. Some years previously a committee of the House of Commons had been appointed to inquire into the matter, and they reported that "the foundation of the lottery system is so radically vicious, that your committee feel convinced that under no system of regulations that can be devised will it be possible for parliament to adopt it as an efficacious source of revenue, and at the same time divest it of all the evils of which it has hitherto been so painful a source." In 1823 the last act that was sanctioned by parliament for the sale of lottery tickets contained provisions for putting down all private lotteries, and for rendering illegal the sale in this country of all tickets in any foreign lottery, a provision which does not even now prevent the circulation of such tickets every now and then by means of the post. Lotteries were absolutely abolished in 1826 in England; a few years later France followed a similar course with regard to her state lotteries, and subsequently they were prohibited by the German states and by Prussia; but the Papal states kept them up. Art-unions, which are supposed to have the effect of cultivating taste, are carried on under a special statute.

CHARLES EDWARD, THE YOUNG PRETENDER.

That son of James Francis Edward, whose birth at Rome in 1720 had again excited the hopes of the Jacobites, was twenty-five years old when the reverses of the English in Flanders and at the battle of Fontenoy led him to imagine that he could not only effect a rising in Scotland, but achieve a victory in England which would secure for him the throne to which he laid claim. Although it had been strongly represented to him that it would be useless to attempt even a rising in the Highlands unless he took with him a force of 6000 disciplined troops and 10,000 stand of arms, he failed to obtain any real assistance from the French, who cared little what became of him; and with £6000 of borrowed money, and such jewels as he could pawn for a further sum, he obtained an eighteen-gun brig, the *Doutelle*,—in which he and the gentlemen who accompanied him embarked,—and an old man-of-war, which carried such arms and ammunition as he had been able to procure. This vessel was disabled after being left to attack a British man-of-war, which had engaged both ships, so that the *Doutelle* with the prince and his companions had to pursue its course alone, and at last came to anchor at an islet between Barra and South Uist.

The romantic story of the hopeless enterprise, which was sustained by the unflinching faithfulness and bravery of the chiefs and their clans; the gathering of the Camerons; the raising of the standard in the vale of Glenfinnan; the treachery to the Government of the old fox Lord Lovat, Macpherson of Cluny, and others who disregarded oaths and obligations; the rapid gathering of the armed bands who marched to Edinburgh; the receptions and balls at Holyrood; the battle of Prestonpans and the disgrace of Cope; the capture of money, stores, and arms; the arrival of aid from France, and the fierce requisitions made by the Highlanders as the army, now better provided, marched onward far across the border: the retreat to Falkirk, and the defeat at Culloden,—has been told a hundred times.

The Pretender had at first to meet only incompetent generals and cowardly opponents, and it was not till his cousin, the Duke of Cumberland, arrived in Edinburgh with his forces that a tragic ending came to this wild enterprise; which, in the fear that it caused of a French invasion, added to an insurrection and the overrunning of the north of England with the horrors of a civil war, called almost the whole country to arms, in a determination to resist the return of the Stuarts to power.

From the first hour that this rash young man landed in Scotland to the battle of Culloden, and the subsequent reprisals by which Cumberland earned the name of "the Butcher," the cause was really hopeless, though even with a scanty, ill-armed, and desultory force so many successes were at first achieved.

Charles Edward, like his father, had a kind of romantic daring, but he lacked the personal courage to retrieve defeat or to pledge his life on the result, to obtain which cost so many brave lives, either on the field, in prison, or on the scaffold. At Culloden the army of the prince, exhausted by hunger, fatigue, and continued marching, were little more than half the number of the army of Cumberland, which was in good condition to take the field. The Highlanders and their French and Irish allies may have been 4000, while their opponents were probably at least 7000 to 8000. The ranks of the rebel army were broken by an attack of the dragoons on their flank. They were outnumbered and out-generalled, and though they fought desperately at first, they began to retreat from the field broken into small parties. Charles fled; and though before the engagement was quite over Lord Elcho implored him to lead a general and desperate charge in person, he turned pale and refused, upon which Elcho called him an Italian coward and scoundrel, and swore he would never serve him or speak to him again: a promise which he kept, although he had to live in exile for the Stuarts' cause.

Of the subsequent wanderings of the prince, who was unable to escape because of the close watch set upon the coast, and therefore kept in hiding in the fastnesses of the Highlands, the tale is romantic and melancholy enough; but it is distinguished chiefly for the courage, fidelity, and exquisite integrity of the poor mountaineers—the hundreds of persons none of whom betrayed him though £30,000 was offered for his apprehension.

It was while he was in hiding in the island of South Uist that Flora Macdonald, a young lady who was the daughter of Macdonald of Milton, undertook to contrive his escape to a safer locality, the island being watched on all sides, while companies of soldiers were searching everywhere for the fugitive. Flora Macdonald was related to Clanronald, the Chevalier's host, who had contrived to conceal him during the month of June, and she was on a visit to the house, where she was distressed day after day by seeing the danger that beset the prince, and by hearing accounts of his condition from his constant attendant O'Neill, who visited the house clandestinely for food and advice.

She expressed an earnest desire to see the prince in person, and declared that if she could in any way save him from his enemies she would do it. Upon this O'Neill ventured to propose that she should take Charles, dressed in woman's clothes, as her maid, and conduct him out of South Uist to Skye. At first Flora Macdonald thought the scheme fantastical and dangerous, and positively declined it; but soon after this conversation means were found to introduce to her, at a solitary farm-house, the prince in person, and then his sad condition, his thin and wasted habit of body, and his arguments went to her heart and removed all scruples, and she went forthwith from this interview to put the scheme into execution. Nobody could possibly leave the island, or escape the cruisers' row-boats and guards, without a passport. Flora asked and obtained from her stepfather, Hugh Macdonald, who commanded part of the troops assembled in South Uist, a pass for herself and her lady's-maid, Betty Burke; and she further induced the captain to recommend to his wife, residing in the Isle of Skye, the said Betty as an excellent spinner of flax and a faithful servant.

We are following Flora Macdonald's own account of the transaction, which is believed to have been written or dictated by herself. It is said there, or rather it is left to be inferred, that her stepfather was not admitted into the dangerous secret, but deceived by Flora's ingenuity; but neither Captain Hugh Macdonald, nor other Macdonalds in South Uist and Skye, were really imposed upon by the young lady. Having obtained the passport, a boat, six boatmen, and some provisions, and sent a dress to Charles, she walked along the sea-shore with Lady Clanronald, and met the proscribed Stuart in his female attire. On the following morning, the weather being calm and serene, Charles, Flora, and the six boatmen set out for Skye. The generous lady and her maid, the prince, landed safe at Mugstole, the seat of the Macdonalds, where Lady Margaret Macdonald was then residing. This lady, who, like her husband, Sir Alexander, had once been a Jacobite of the deepest hue, gave the lady and her mock maid a good dinner, and, as her house was open to the visits of officers and troops, she sent them forward to her kinsman and factor, Macdonald of Kingsburgh, more in the interior of the island. Near to this place the Chevalier put on a Highland dress, and then Flora left him to the care of Kingsburgh, and went home to her stepfather's house.

The day after his arrival at Kingsburgh's house in Skye the Chevalier left that island and went over to the small island of Rasay, which was only six miles off. The chief, Macleod of Rasay, who had fought for the Pretender both at Falkirk and Culloden, was lying hid somewhere on the mainland, but his sons were at home, and they accommodated Charles in a cowshed. They had no better lodging to give him—there was nothing better left on the island; for a detachment of King George's army had been there a few days before with fire and sword, had carried off all the cattle and burned every house in Rasay. While the Chevalier was lying pinched with hunger in the cowshed at Rasay, his generous deliverer, Flora Macdonald, was apprehended by some of the militia in Skye, put on board a king's ship, and carried as a prisoner and dangerous rebel to London. Her secret had been forced from the poor boatmen who had ferried her and Charles from South Uist. Kingsburgh also was laid in durance, and threatened with nothing less than death.

Still the Pretender roamed through the Isle of Skye, whither he had sought to escape from the troops who were watching every ravine and pass. Here he was conducted through the wildest part of the country, and at length found a refuge with a company of freebooters who dwelt in a cave, and *lifted* not only cattle for his food but the baggage of the officers of Fort Augustus, in order to provide him with clothes and clean linen. At last, after above five weeks, the

royal fugitive became tired of this concealment, and Peter Grant, one of the seven men of the cave, went at imminent risk into Lochaber, where he found the brave chief, Cameron of Clunes, who sent word back that he would meet the prince at the head of Glenquoich, where he had a little hut in a secret place.

In the state in which matters now were, the wisest and best thing to do was to scare the wretched fugitive back to France —to permit and connive at Charles' escape. George II. was not a bloodthirsty prince, and even if his nature had been more severe he would not have chosen to draw down upon himself the odium of Europe and the criticism of every civilized court, by putting to death as a felon and traitor the descendant of many kings. To have kept Charles as a state prisoner either in Scotland or England, or even in the American plantations, would have been very troublesome, and might have proved extremely dangerous. For the safety, for the honour of the house of Brunswick, it was better to let him go than to catch him; probably this was the opinion of a considerable portion of the English cabinet, and of not a few of the officers that were serving in Scotland.

Charles instantly left the cave and travelled along the tops of the mountains in a very stormy night; but as he thought it necessary to lie concealed by day, he did not reach Glenquoich and the little hut at the time appointed, and when he got there he found neither the chief nor food to eat. Peter Grant, however, supplied both these deficiences: he killed a deer and found out Clunes again, who forthwith came to the hut with his three sons. The chief informed Charles, who wanted to get to Badenoch, where the gentle Lochiel and Cluny were lurking, that the troops and scouts of government were exceedingly numerous, and that all the ferries of the rivers and lochs were so strictly guarded that a journey was for the present impossible.

It was therefore resolved to keep close for a time in or about the little hut in Glenquoich. They were in this situation when Macdonald of Lochgary, and Dr. Cameron, Lochiel's own brother, penetrated into the district in search of the prince; for Lochiel and Cluny had both concluded that he must be somewhere to the north of the lakes. These two gentlemen found out Charles, and after many more dangers and hardships they succeeded in conveying him to Badenoch, where, at a place called Mellanauir, he met Lochiel and Cluny. The gentle

Lochiel was still lame, and suffering from the wounds he had received in the battle of Culloden. After staying a day or two in the hut called Uiskchibra, the two chiefs conducted the prince to a still better hiding-place in the great mountains of Benalder, on the banks of Loch Ericht, which Cluny had fitted up some months before for his own use and that of his wounded friend. It was very appropriately called the "cage."

"The cage," says Cluny, "was no larger than to contain six or seven persons, four of whom were frequently employed playing at cards, one idle looking on, one baking, and another firing bread and cooking." Here the party remained caged till the 13th of September, when a message arrived from Cameron of Clunes to inform Charles that two French frigates had put into Lochnanuagh, and were waiting there to convey him and his friends off. The Chevalier set out immediately, but as he only travelled by night he did not arrive at the port till the 19th. Other messages had warned other gentlemen lying in concealment up and down the country; and besides Lochiel, Cluny, and Colonel Roy Stuart, about one hundred embarked with Charles on the 20th of September, and thence proceeded to Paris. But before this time many of those who had ventured for him had been hanged and beheaded, with the usual and revolting accompaniments of drawing and quartering; and afterwards, while Charles was showing his face in the French opera, the heads of braver and better men were exhibited at Temple Bar, on the walls of Carlisle, York, and other places.[1]

Flora Macdonald was released after twelve months' confinement, and went back to the Highlands with some £1500 in her pocket, which had been collected for her chiefly among Jacobite ladies in London. She afterwards married the son of Kingsburgh. At the time when she smuggled the Young Pretender in her train she was about twenty-four years old. Dr. Johnson saw her in the year 1773, when Boswell contrived to get the great moralist to the Highlands and to the Isle of Skye. Flora, or as she spelled her name, Flory, was then past her seventh climacteric; but Johnson describes her as "not old, of a pleasing person and elegant behaviour;" and his companion, Boswell, sets her down as "a little woman, of a genteel appearance, and uncommonly mild and well bred." Johnson says, in

[1] *Comprehensive History of England.*

RELICS OF PRINCE CHARLES EDWARD,

THE YOUNG PRETENDER.

1. Folding Spoon and Case; in the possession of Joseph Mayer, Esq., F.S.A., Liverpool.
2. Dress Sword; in her Majesty's Collection, Windsor Castle.
3. Silver-hilted Broadsword; in the possession of the Duchess of Gordon.
4. Silver Goblet; preserved in Castle Cluny, Scotland.
5. Travelling (folding) Knife, Fork, and Spoon.
6. Shield.
7. Sporran.
8. Dirk. } Preserved in Castle Cluny, Scotland.
9. and 10. Pistols.

RELICS OF PRINCE CHARLES EDWARD.

a letter to Mrs. Thrale, "She was carried to London, but dismissed without a trial, and came down with Malcolm Macleod, against whom sufficient evidence could not be procured. She and her husband are poor, and are now going to try their fortune in America—Sic rerum volvitur orbis." They did emigrate to America, but returned to Scotland during the war of independence, and Flora died in the Isle of Skye on the 4th of March, 1790.

Since the time of Œdipus no royal line has equalled that of the Stuarts in its calamities. The first James, adorned with the graces of poetry and chivalry, a wise legislator, a sagacious and resolute king, perished in his forty-fourth year. His son, the second James, was killed in his thirtieth year at the siege of Roxburgh Castle, by the bursting of a cannon. The third James, after the battle of Sauchieburn, in which his rebellious subjects were countenanced and aided by his own son, was stabbed, in his thirty-sixth year, beneath a humble roof by a pretended priest. That son, the chivalrous madman of Flodden, compassed his own death and that of the flower of his kingdom, while only forty years of age, by a foolish knight-errantry. At an age ten years younger his only son, James V., died of a broken heart. Over the suffering and follies, if we may not say crimes, and over the mournful and unwarrantable doom of the beauteous Mary, the world will never cease to debate. Her grandson expiated at Whitehall, by a bloody death, the errors induced by his self-will and his pernicious education. The second Charles, the Merry Monarch, had a fate as sad as any of his ancestors; for though he died in his bed, his life was that of a heartless voluptuary, who had found in his years of seeming prosperity neither truth in man nor fidelity in woman. His brother, the bigot James, lost three kingdoms and disinherited the dynasty, for his blind adherence to a faith that failed to regulate his life. The Old Pretender was a cipher, and the Young Pretender, after a youthful flash of promise, passed a useless life, and ended it as a drunken dotard. The last of the race, Henry, Cardinal York, died in 1804, a spiritless old man, and a pensioner of that house of Hanover against which his father and brother had waged war with no advantage to themselves, and with the forfeiture of life and lands, of liberty and country, to many of the noblest and most chivalrous inhabitants of our island.[1]

[1] *Fraser's Magazine.*

THE DEATH OF GENERAL WOLFE, 1759.

Walpole had lost his influence, and all the power of the government seemed to be in the hands of Pitt, the first Earl of Chatham. Louis XV. was defeated and impoverished, and it was time to make another decided effort against those Canadian possessions which were still held by the French, and where we had hitherto been unsuccessful in our attempts to make them our own. For this enterprise Pitt determined to put forward a *protégée* of his own, a young major-general, James Wolfe, who had already distinguished himself no less by his courage and ability, than by the perfect discipline which he had introduced into his regiment—the 67th—which took a prominent part at Minden.

The Canadian campaign was so arranged that Wolfe was to advance with a part of our forces and seize Quebec, the capital of the French provinces; General Amherst, with a second division, was to occupy Crown Point, reduce Fort Ticonderoga, then cross Lake Champlain, fall down the St. Lawrence, and join Wolfe under the walls of Quebec; while General Prideaux, with a third division and a considerable body of wild Indians, was to invest Niagara, then embark on Lake Ontario, besiege and carry Montreal, and then form his junction with Wolfe and Amherst under the capital. These combined movements had generally failed, even when natural obstacles were far less numerous, and the distances to be traversed by the different corps far shorter; and when Wolfe got near to Quebec he found himself alone with the division he had brought.

About the last day in June Wolfe disembarked his troops upon the large and fertile island of Orleans, a little below Quebec. Here he erected some batteries, which Montcalm, the French general, vainly attempted to prevent by throwing a strong detachment across the river. Wolfe also prepared a military hospital and works to secure his stores. He attempted to reconcile the Canadians on the island by friendly proclamation; but those rough people joined scalping parties of wild Indians that were skulking among the woods, and butchered all the English stragglers they could surprise. While the fleet lay at the isle of Orleans it was exposed to great danger; and if once the fleet had been destroyed, or even driven from its post, nothing would have remained for Wolfe but a surrender. The troops were scarcely landed when a terrible storm blew down the river, driving several of our large ships from their anchors, and making the transports run foul of one another. Some of the smaller craft foundered, and a considerable number of boats were swamped. While they were in this confusion the enemy sent down from Quebec seven fire-ships towards the thickest part of our shipping; but the British sailors grappled them, towed them away to the banks, and left them fast aground, where they lay burning to the water's edge without doing any mischief; and some radeaux or rafts piled up with combustible materials, and sent down after the fire-ships had failed, were treated in the same manner by our seamen, who behaved with admirable spirit.

Quebec by this time was strongly fortified, and its natural situation always rendered it formidable to an assailant, for it stands on a steep rock at the confluence of the St. Charles and St. Lawrence, and these rivers, rocks, and ravines render it inaccessible on three of its sides. Montcalm, as brave an officer as Wolfe, covered the town with 10,000 men, having posted himself on the left bank of the St. Charles with encampments extending as far as the river Montmorenci, and with entrenchments thrown up at every accessible place. With an inferior force Wolfe resolved to attack Montcalm in this position. "When," he says in a letter to Pitt, "that succours of all kinds had been thrown into Quebec, that five battalions of regular troops, some of the troops of the colony, and every Canadian that was able to bear arms, besides several nations of savages, had taken the field in a very advantageous position, I could not flatter myself that I should be able to reduce the place. I sought, however, an occasion to attack their army, knowing well that with these troops I was able to fight, and that a victory might disperse them."

At last, on the 31st of July, Wolfe assailed Montcalm in his entrenchments. Leaving Brigadier Townshend to ford the Montmorenci and attack in flank, Wolfe, with the help of the ships and their boats, threw himself on the beach and attacked in front. The *Centurion* man-of-war was so placed as to check the fire of a French battery which commanded the ford of the Montmorenci, and two transports drawing little water were furnished with guns and sent close in shore to cover the spot which Wolfe had selected for his landing; but these two vessels, light as they were, could not get near enough to be of much use; a number of boats crowded with soldiers grounded upon a ledge of rocks, time was lost in getting them off, and Wolfe was obliged to send an officer to stop Townshend, who was already crossing the ford. The French, meanwhile, had united their artillery on the point menaced—a rising ground beyond the river bank—and galled by their fire, the English grenadiers, so soon as they were landed, rushed tumultuously up to the formidable entrenchments without waiting for the corps which were to sustain them and join in the attack. In fact, Townshend, though steadily upon his march, and perfectly in order, was still at some distance; and Brigadier Monckton had not got his men out of the boats. The grenadiers were met in the teeth by a fire too terrible for the bravest of them, and they fell back in confusion after sustaining a serious loss. Still further deterred by the approach of night, and the ominous roaring of the St. Lawrence, for the mighty tide was now ebbing and a storm was setting in, Wolfe gave up the attack, and withdrew his brave men. "The French," he says, "did not attempt to interrupt us; but some of their savages came down to murder such wounded as could not be brought off, and to scalp the dead as their custom is."

Wolfe's situation now seemed almost desperate, and his health began to fail him. In a letter to Pitt, written from his head-quarters at Montmorenci more than a month after this failure, he confessed that he had descended to the dubiousness and despondency of consulting a council of war. "I found myself so ill," said he, "and am still so weak, that I begged the general officers to consult together for the public utility. To the uncommon strength of this country, the enemy have added, for the defence of the river, a great number of floating batteries and boats. By the vigilance of these, and the Indians round our posts, it has been impossible to execute anything by surprise. We have almost the whole force of Canada to oppose. In this situation there is such a choice of difficulties, that I own myself at a loss how to determine. The affairs of Great Britain require the most vigorous measures, but then the courage of a handful of brave men should be exerted only where there is some hope of a favourable event."

He declared that he would rather die than be brought to a court-martial for miscarrying; and in conjunction with Admiral Saunders, he concerted a plan for scaling the Heights of Abraham, and gaining possession of the elevated plateau at the back of Quebec, where the fortifications were the weakest, as the French engineers had there trusted to the precipices and the broad river beneath. In order to deceive the enemy, the admiral sailed some three or four leagues higher up the river, lay there as if with some other intention, and then, on the night of the 12th of September, glided down the river, and put out all his boats to land the troops under the Heights of Abraham. Through the darkness of the night, and the skill and caution of the seamen, the French outposts and sentinels were all passed without disturbance, and the English soldiers were landed at the appointed spot by boatfuls at a time. The first that landed were some nimble Highlanders, who climbed the steep face of the rock like goats. The English light infantry followed the Highlanders, and were in their turn followed by the troops of the line. There was a French guard over their heads, and hearing a rustling noise, but seeing nothing, these fellows fired down the precipices at random. Our men then fired up into the air, and also at random; but terrified at so strange and unexpected an attempt, the French picket ran off, all but the captain, who was wounded and taken prisoner, and who begged our officers to sign a certificate of his courage and steadiness, lest he should be punished as a traitor, since the English general's bold enterprise would be believed impossible without corruption and connivance.

Wolfe now stood on the long-desired Heights of Abraham. He had no artillery with him, and excessive fatigue and disease, the French and the wild Indians, had reduced his army to less than 5000 men. His light infantry, however, seized four guns which the French had placed in battery, and the English sailors, by dint of extraordinary exertions, hauled up one gun from the landing-place. On the other side, Montcalm came on in too great a hurry to allow the French to wait for their artillery, and they brought up no more than two small field-pieces.

At first the French general could hardly credit the evidence of his senses; so impossible did it seem for an army to have ascended those dangerous cliffs. At last he said, "I see them where they ought not to be; but since they are there, we must fight. I will go and crush them." Quitting his entrenchments, he advanced with confident haste to the field where Wolfe had already formed his little army in order of battle, within long cannon-shot range of the outworks of Quebec. After lining the bushes with detachments of Indians, the French and Canadians advanced, as if to charge, in very good order, and with great vivacity; but they opened an irregular fire before they got within musket-range. The English reserved their fire until the enemy were within a few yards of their front, and then they poured in a terrible discharge. This first volley was succeeded by a most steady, deliberate, and sustained fire, and in less than half an hour the French and Canadians began to waver. As Wolfe stood conspicuous in the front line, cheering his men, a musket-ball struck his wrist. He wrapped a handkerchief round the wound, and soon put himself at the head of his grenadiers, who had fixed their bayonets for the charge. He was hit by a second ball in the upper part of the abdomen; but he seemed scarcely to heed this more serious wound, and was in the act of cheering the grenadiers when a third musket-ball hit him and brought him to the ground. His grieved men picked him up and carried him to the rear. He was dying fast, yet he still continued intent on the battle. As his eyes were growing dim he heard a wounded officer near him exclaim, "See how they run!" "Who run?" cried Wolfe. "The French," replied the officer; "they give way in all directions." "Then," said the hero, "I die content!"—and after giving an order for Webb's regiment to move down to Charles's River and secure the bridge there in order to cut off the enemy's retreat, he calmly expired on the ground among his officers and faithful soldiers.

General Monckton, the second in command, was dangerously wounded, but Townshend nobly and speedily completed the victory. General Montcalm received a mortal wound in attempting to rally the discomfited French, and his second in command was made prisoner, and so badly wounded, that he died on the following day. The city of Quebec capitulated five days after the action, and the disheartened remnant of the French army of Canada retired to Montreal, where they could not maintain themselves. In effect the project of Pitt was realized, and one battle gave us the dominion of that immense country. One despatch conveyed to England intelligence of the unexpected victory on the Heights of Abraham, of the death of Wolfe, and of the surrender of Quebec.

GEORGE THE THIRD.

The character of George III. cannot be justly estimated without reference to two conditions, which must considerably modify our opinion. First, the circumstances attending his early training and education; and secondly, the mental aberration to which he was liable, and to which he succumbed at intervals, even before the severe attack which, in 1810, made it necessary for him to be secluded from society, and left the throne no more than a name, and the government in the hands of the ministry. After the death of his father, Prince George was brought up entirely under the influence of his mother, and had little companionship but that of waiting-women and grooms of the household. If it was thought probable that the restrictions to which he was subject would have the effect of rendering him pliable and easily influenced by those who ought to take the upper hand when he came to the throne, there never was a greater error. It soon became evident that he had all the obstinacy of his grandfather without much of his ability, but with a great deal of his courage and pertinacity.

For a short time Lord Waldegrave was his "governor," and seems to have had a complete insight into his character. He says, "He is strictly honest, but wants that frank and open behaviour which makes honesty appear amiable. When he had a very scanty allowance it was one of his favourite maxims that men should be just before they are generous; his income is now very considerably augmented, but his generosity has not increased in equal proportion. His religion is free from all hypocrisy, but is not of the most charitable sort; he has rather too much attention to the sins of his neighbour. He has spirit, but not of the active kind; and does not want resolution, but it is mixed with too much obstinacy. He has great command of his passions, and will seldom do wrong, except when he mistakes wrong for right; but as often as this shall happen it will be difficult to undeceive him, because he is uncommonly indolent and has strong prejudices. His want of application and aversion to business would be far less dangerous was he eager in the pursuit of pleasure, for the transition from pleasure to business is both shorter and easier than from a state of total inaction. He has a kind of unhappiness in his temper, which if it be not conquered before it has taken too deep a root will be a source of frequent anxiety. Whenever he is displeased his anger does not break out into heat and violence, but he becomes sullen and silent, and retires to his closet, not to compose his mind by study or contemplation, but merely to indulge the melancholy enjoyment of his own ill humour. Even when the fit is ended, unfavourable symptoms very frequently return, which indicate that on certain occasions his royal highness has too correct a memory. Though I have mentioned his good and bad qualities without flattery and without aggravation, allowances should still be made on account of his youth and his bad education; for though the Bishop of Peterborough (Dr. John Thomas), now Bishop of Salisbury, the preceptor; Mr. Stone, sub-governor; and Mr. Scott, the sub-preceptor, were men of sense, men of learning, and worthy good men, they had but little weight and influence. The mother and the nursery always prevailed. During the course of the last year there has indeed been some alteration; the authority of the nursery has gradually declined, and the Earl of Bute, by the assistance of the mother, has now the entire confidence."

This estimate of character, which reads almost like the professed diagnosis of a modern phrenologist, was so shrewd that it will fairly illustrate the obstinacy, the parsimony, the sullenness, the general conscientiousness, the self-assertion, and even the arbitrary determination of the king, who during a long reign, till the time that he disappeared from public affairs in 1810, contrived to get so much of his own way that the country was again under the personal rule of the throne, or was governed in turns by a sovereign who occasionally thwarted his cabinet, and by able ministers who were strong enough to control him. It is even now difficult to understand how large a part this common-place, obstinate, and prejudiced man took in public affairs during years when England had to hold a foremost place while the continent of Europe was in the throes of revolution, and when her own great and growing colony of America was irritated into an armed resistance which resulted in unexpected separation and a declaration of its national independence.

The education of George III. when he was Prince of Wales was bad enough. His mother had continually kept him within the narrow compass of her own small and tyrannical disposition that she and Bute

might have the power to rule. But in order to assume this power more effectually she had taught him that he was above the interference of parliaments and ministries; and he was so ready to accept this lesson, that, directly he came to the throne, he began to act for himself. For some time he continued to be guided by Bute, and the country often resented the interference of this unpopular minister; but Bute could neither restrain the arrogance of his pupil nor initiate a policy which would be acceptable to the nation, and he ultimately disappeared from the political arena. This disappearance, however, was only just in time to save the country from a conflict with the throne, for Bute's endeavour to raise the royal prerogative was so near raising a revolution that he retired in terror from the hatred of the people and in fear lest he had involved the king in ruin. It is impossible here even to indicate the tremendous series of events amidst which successive administrations had to contend for the position which England maintained after protracted political struggles and repeated wars, but the relative position of the people and the political leaders is to be gathered from the lampoons, the caricatures, and the broadsides that were constantly issued, and the coarseness and vituperation of which are amazing to us, who live under a wider constitutional freedom, and a more regular administration in which the mass of the people are acquiring a decided influence.

The king himself was a most diligent man of business. No permanent secretary ever knew more, few half so much, of the minutiæ of official life and the *personnel* of the civil and other services. "George III. worked as hard as a government clerk is supposed to work, and his interest in such bureaucratic details corresponds well with the type of his intellect. With two or three fixed ideas, or rather prejudices, held and pursued with the intensity of monomania, he had neither the capacity nor the inclination to form any wide or elevated views. His education had been grossly neglected, or rather he had been allowed or encouraged to neglect it, and his mind, sharp and retentive, but narrow and essentially unphilosophical, contented itself within a sphere as narrow as it was well explored. His idea of personal government was that of not being thwarted in his own wishes, and of knowing and sanctioning everything that was done. He had severe ideas of discipline and legal and official authority, and nothing must be done to unduly relax the one or to weaken the other. He had a horror of popular politics and popular interference in government, except in support of the rights and under the leadership of the crown. He was fond of the lower orders in their proper place; he loved to mix familiarly with them in the spirit of paternal condescension in which a German potentate chats with a peasant; but he resented all independent action or thought on their part as subversive of authority and government. He wished them to be paid and fed according to their condition, and educated in a manner appropriate to the state of life 'unto which it had pleased God to call them.' He had a sincere and strong desire for the happiness of his people and the welfare of the nation: but it was essential that there should be a general spirit of subordination, the proper and necessary amount of taxes duly paid, and the full number of persons, young and old, as determined by the fixed processes of justice, whipped, imprisoned, or hung every year, if government was to be carried on at all. All ideas beyond these were sedition and anarchy.

During two periods of his life George III. had the opportunity of putting these ideas of order and justice into operation. In 1770 he found in Lord North a pliant though not always a sympathizing agent of his views, and everyone knows how disastrous was the personal administration of that period: how incapable was the administration at home, and how disastrous the events abroad which robbed us of an empire. In the younger Pitt no doubt George III. expected to meet with a second pliant tool, like the easy-tempered North; but he met with a mind which, though compliant on many points with the royal prejudices, to the injury of his lasting reputation as a statesman, had naturally as stiff and proud a nature as his own, and was as little satisfied with the name without the reality of power. The king could not venture to order about such a man in the insolent manner in which he had treated George Granville, and he was wise enough to perceive this. The result was a tacit compromise, by which the king for many years always consulted Mr. Pitt, was much influenced by his views, and left him a considerable share of administrative power and influence; but by which Mr. Pitt, on his side, gave up all idea of a really great domestic and foreign policy, in deference to the king's rooted prejudices. The French revolution greatly assisted king and minister in holding their own against all opponents, by annihilating the Whig party, and driving the terrified nation into a fanatic admiration of the personal government of the sovereign. Every needful reform was refused or postponed indefinitely, and people were educated into a state of public abuses and general jobbery and corruption as the normal condition of life. It has tasked all the ability and energies of the statesmen of William IV. and Victoria to remedy the effects of this long maladministration."[1]

WASHINGTON CROSSING THE DELAWARE, 1776.

Amidst the momentous events which distinguished the reign of George III., the most important to the history of the world was the declaration of independence by the Americans and the separation of that great colony from British government. It would be impossible within our present limits even to trace the outlines of those successive misunderstandings which led to repeated hostilities and the final severance of the two nations; but it is remarkable that while the duplicity of Benjamin Franklin and some other leaders of the democratic section of Americans hastened on a separation which they pretended to deprecate, the settlement of the republic was achieved by George Washington, a loyal and honest Virginian gentleman, who, having in his youth emerged from the quiet life of a country squire or land-owner to command a militia regiment, became the successful general of the American forces and the first magistrate of the States which overthrew and abandoned British rule.

While Franklin, their agent in England, was still professing a desire for pacification, and before the Earl of Chatham had proposed his "provisional bill for settling the troubles in America," a measure which would have been rejected by the insurgent Americans as it was rejected by the British House of Lords, the Bostonians, the Virginians, and the states which had joined their confederacy, were already committed to hostilities. While the Houses of Parliament in England had been echoing with the sonorous periods of oratory, the hill sides and river banks of America had been ringing with sharp and dissonant peals of musketry. The colonists had fired their first shot, and blood had

[1] Sanford. *Estimates of the English Kings.*

been flowing in no diminutive stream. They had passed the winter in making preparations for the General Congress which was to meet at Philadelphia in the month of May, in fabricating and preparing arms, in drilling the militia, and in keeping up their spirits by the production and interchange of irritating manifestoes and proclamations. Washington, like the majority of the revolted American people, had maintained his loyalty both to the crown and to the mother country, and had demanded only that the colony should not be subjected to heavy taxation by the British government, but should regulate its own fiscal burdens by the votes of the state assemblies. Even when actual hostilities had commenced he seems to have thought that a determined attitude, and a demonstration of the ability of the Americans to withstand the demands made upon them by force of arms, would lead to the repeal of obnoxious measures, and the return of the states to their allegiance under just and favourable conditions.

It is not easy to determine that this was the opinion of Jefferson, Samuel Adams, and the other leaders, and it is quite certain that a number of the men who exercised considerable influence, intended from the first to revive republican sentiments, and to do all that lay in their power to commit the country to a republic. The reverses to the American forces which for some time followed were themselves instrumental in bringing about the final result. The generals who were sent out against the colonists were themselves so inefficient, that only the ignorance of those to whom they were opposed on the subject of military strategy could have enabled them to claim the advantages which they gained; and the result was an increasing determination on the part of the insurgents, which at length took the shape of an almost general resolve on the part of the insurgent states, to fight not so much for colonial as for national independence.

As late as the 9th of October, 1774, Washington wrote to a friend serving in the king's army: "You are taught to believe that the people of Massachusetts are rebellious; setting up for independency, and what not; give me leave to tell you, my good friend, that you are abused . . . give me leave to add, and I think I can announce it as a fact, that it is not the wish or interest of that government or any other upon this continent, separately or collectively, to set up for independence." A little more than two years afterwards, when a series of engagements and reverses had been accompanied by repeated divisions, difficulties,

and disaffections which had almost threatened to break up and divide the colony, Washington himself, who had long been in command of the revolutionary army, was crossing the Delaware after reverses which his courage more than his generalship enabled him to overcome.

After the accession of Georgia to the rebellious states Congress had assumed the style of "the thirteen united provinces;" and not only were means of communication opened up, but a post-office was established between Falmouth in Massachusetts and Savannah in Georgia, the postmaster being Benjamin Franklin, who had returned to aid them in their organizations. The battle of Bunker's Hill had been fought, and the Americans were short both of muskets and gunpowder, they were also without tents, and had no supplies of shoes and clothing. Washington soon obtained fresh supplies from Congress, and the dilatoriness and fatuity of the English generals allowed him time to procure powder from New Jersey and other places, while the appointment of a commissary-general insured a better provision of the means of living. General Gage had been recalled from Boston, General Howe taking the chief command. The coast was swarming with privateers, which waged a desultory warfare with English ships.

The American forces soon began to retrieve some of the previous disasters. They made advances on the town, and besieged the British army there by well-executed stratagems. Gage and Howe had neglected to occupy the hills, which their opponents successively converted into points of attack which commanded the town, and from which they drove away the British floating batteries from their stations. Howe had already received instructions to evacuate Boston and to proceed to New York; but before he commenced to move, the Americans began the bombardment of the British position, and after ineffectual and feeble attempts to dislodge them he was obliged to make a compromise by which he was permitted to leave with his troops, in return for his promise to abstain from burning and destroying the town.

Yet if the British generals had exhibited incapacity when they were at Boston, Washington displayed little greater ability after Howe had taken his troops to New York. The American army under their brave general could prevent the British forces from operating successfully at different places at the same time, but the contest itself was prolonged and difficult. It must be admitted, however, that the people of New York as a whole were so little in favour of the Congress that after severe fighting, and the danger of losing half his army, which he had placed on Long Island, but which both the general and admiral were too slow to shut up there, as they might have done, Washington found it impossible to defend the city, and evacuated it when the British were just closing around him on all sides. Howe had scarcely taken possession of it when a conflagration, commencing from different points, destroyed a large portion of buildings, and would have spread but for the soldiers, who were beat to quarters, and the sailors from the fleet, who succeeded in putting it out with great difficulty. Of course the fire was the work of incendiaries, many of whom were taken and killed, and might have been regarded as martyrs, had it not been that New York was unfavourable to the Congress, and that the property was destroyed by those who had little sympathy either for the entering army or the abiding royalists.

Washington then took up his position on White Plains, and from White Plains retreated to Croton River, taking up a position at North Castle. Fort Washington and King's Bridge were carried with the loss of a large contingent of Washington's army. On the 18th of November Lord Cornwallis crossed the Hudson, drove the Americans from the remaining forts, and advanced into the Jerseys. Washington then fell back on the Delaware River. After raising reinforcements Cornwallis marched on towards Brunswick, and Washington determined to attack Trenton, which was held by a brigade of German mercenaries. It was a bold undertaking to attempt to cross the Delaware; but on Christmas night (1766) he embarked in a storm of snow and sleet, leading his small force of 2400 men and 20 cannon by boats through the floating ice. At daylight they had reached Trenton, which they attacked by two divisions. The garrison, alarmed by the firing on the outer picket line, hastily formed and began to advance; but their commander was mortally wounded, and the American columns converged upon them, charged into their ranks, and seized their artillery. In this charge the Americans suffered some casualties. Lieutenant Monroe, afterwards president of the United States, was wounded, but the ranks of the garrison force were broken and a panic soon spread amongst them. Six hundred of the Germans escaped, but 1000 were made prisoners; while the colours of the Anspach, Kuyphausen, and Rall regiments were captured. This success led to the investment of New Jersey, by which the position of Washington was better secured and his ultimate achievements supported.

DEATH OF MAJOR PIERSON, 1782.

The reign of George III. was one long contest not only in the political arena, where factions were fierce and party spirit ran high, but by the relation which England was compelled to sustain towards the rest of Europe. We were continually at war, and on some occasions appeared to rush into conflict against half the world. The protracted struggle in America was accompanied with hostilities in the East and the West Indies, with France and with Spain either separately or as allies, and at last with France, Spain, and the American republican forces, to support which the corrupt government and the doomed monarchy of France were oppressing the half-famished peasantry by new taxes and almost unbearable imposts.

It was after the battle of Ushant, and after the pirate Paul Jones had attempted his expedition on the Scottish coast with a mixed squadron of French, Spanish, and American vessels, that an attack was made upon the island of Jersey by the Baron de Rullecourt; an invasion that would have been successful had there been no braver and more determined defender than Major Corbet, the lieutenant-governor of the island. On two former occasions attempts had been made to gain possession of the island, first in May, 1779, when an armament with a force of above 5000 men under the Prince of Nassau was repulsed and had to relinquish the enterprise, and again when the French fleet was defeated by Sir James Wallace.

This third effort was in December, 1780, and the Baron de Rullecourt, who perhaps had been informed of the character of the lieutenant-governor and of the small force likely to be brought to oppose a landing, contrived to disembark 700 men, and took possession of St. Heliers, where he succeeded in taking Major Corbet prisoner, and causing him to sign a capitulation surrendering the island. But both the invader and the cowardly lieutenant-governor had misjudged the spirit of the troops and the people, who were influenced by the patriotic insubordination of Major Pierson, a gallant officer, who was second in command, and refusing to acknowledge the capitulation, summoned all the troops and island militia whom he could collect in the market-place of St.

Heliers, and at once attacked the French, being assisted by the townspeople, who kept up a fusilade from the houses. The engagement was short, sharp, and decisive; a number of the invaders were killed, and the remainder surrendered, the Baron de Rullecourt himself having been so severely wounded that he died almost immediately, while the gallant young Pierson was killed by the last shot fired by the French.

NELSON BOARDING THE *SAN JOSEF* AT THE BATTLE OF ST. VINCENT (1797).

It was sixteen years after the attempt to capture the island of Jersey. All the momentous events which had been agitating Europe had been dwarfed for a time by the stupendous horrors of the French Revolution and the Reign of Terror. Rodney, Hood, and Howe had successively maintained the supremacy of England in maritime warfare, and now that Bonaparte was at the head of the army of France, and had vain or vague thoughts of an invasion of Britain, the approaching conflicts which were to mark the later years of the reign of George III. were to be discerned both by statesmen and commanders. There had been mutiny in the English navy, and yet its prestige had not suffered when it had to fight the enemies of the country. Duncan's victory at Camperdown had given such good proof of this, that an improvement in the condition of the sailors, and the proclamation of a general pardon to the mutineers of the Nore after the ring-leaders had been punished, improved the spirit and discipline of the navy, enabled us to contend against the combined fleets of France, Holland, and Spain, and prepared for the series of victories which brought Nelson into the foremost place while he was serving under Admiral Sir John Jervis.

It was on the 14th of February, 1797, that the Mediterranean fleet, under this commander, fell in, off Cape St. Vincent, with the great Spanish fleet just come out of Cadiz under the command of Don José de Cordova. Sir John, beside his own ship the *Victory*, had two vessels of 100 guns, three of 98 guns, nine of 74 guns, to one of which (the *Captain*) Commodore Nelson had exchanged that he might be in the

line of battle; one 64-gun ship, and three 32-gun frigates. The Spanish force comprised the flag-ship, 130 guns, six of 112 guns, among which was the *San Josef*, two of 89 guns, four of 74 guns, twelve frigates, and one brig. The difference was serious, but with such a commander and such captains as Nelson, Trowbridge, Collingwood, Saumarez, Towry, and Calder, Englishmen were not likely to regard it with much anxiety. As the dawn of day showed the strength of the enemy, Calder reported the numbers of the vessels which came in sight. "Ten sail of the line, Sir John." "Very well, sir." "Fifteen sail of the line, Sir John." "Very well, sir." "Twenty sail of the line, Sir John." "Very well, sir." "Twenty-seven sail of the line, Sir John; against such a force is it advisable to ——." "Enough, sir, enough," broke in the stern old admiral; "were there fifty sail of the line, sir, I'd go through them all."

Trowbridge led the attack after the opening fire of the British ship *Culloden*; and it is said that the admiral, when he watched the seaman-like skill with which the captain manœuvred, exclaimed, "Look, look at Trowbridge! does he not manœuvre as if all England was looking at him? Would to God all England were present to appreciate as I do the gallant captain of the *Culloden*." At about half-past twelve the leading ship of the lee division of the Spaniards, bearing the flag of Vice-admiral Moreno, made an effort to cut the British line ahead of the *Victory*, which was nearly the centre ship; but Sir John Jervis was not to be deceived, and at once opened such a tremendous fire that his antagonist was compelled to tack and abandon the attempt. The commander-in-chief's flag-ship then opened a raking fire upon the remaining ships of this division, which compelled all but one of them to wear round and bear up.

At a quarter to one o'clock the *Victory* tacked, in order to follow up the main body of the Spanish fleet, and a few minutes later Admiral de Cordova bore up to join the ships to leeward. Commodore Nelson, whose ship was in the rear of the line, immediately discovered the Spanish admiral's design, and disregarding the signal flying on the flagship that the ships were to tack in succession, gave the order to wear ship, so that the *Captain*, passing between the *Diadem* and the *Excellent*, the two rearmost ships, threw herself directly in the way of the huge Spanish four-decker. The Spanish admiral, thus thwarted, again hauled up on the larboard tack, but the *Captain* overtook and engaged her till Trowbridge came up in the *Culloden*, when Nelson pushed on into the thick of the fight, which soon became general. Collingwood was soon after him, after having taken one of the enemy's vessels, and leaving another to be dealt with by the *Orion*. Very soon the *Captain* was little better than a wreck, but it was a victorious wreck. She had lost her fore-top-mast; she had not a sail, shroud, or rope left her which was not shot away; and she was incapable of further service in the line or in chase. She was hotly engaged with the *San Nicolas* of 80 guns, when Collingwood in the *Excellent* came onward between the two vessels, and while allowing the crew of the *Captain* to replenish the shot-lockers, poured a broadside into the enemy and passed on. In luffing to avoid this fire the *San Nicolas* ran foul of the *San Josef*, which had lost her mizen-mast. The *Captain* renewed the combat, but her fore-top-mast was gone over the side, and it was necessary for Nelson either to take some decisive action, or to drop out of the battle with his crippled ship. His resolve was soon taken, and putting the *Captain's* helm a-starboard he ran foul of the 80-gun ship, with her port cat-head striking the starboard quarter and her sprit-sail yard hooking the mizen-rigging. Meanwhile the *San Josef's* main-yard was locked in the fore-rigging of the *San Nicolas*, and it was necessary to take both or neither.

Nelson himself thus describes the achievement:—" The soldiers of the 69th (doing duty as marines), with an alacrity which will ever do them credit, and Lieutenant Pearson of the same regiment, were almost the foremost on this service. The first man who jumped into the enemy's mizen-chains was Captain Berry, late my first lieutenant (Captain Miller was in the very act of going also, but I directed him to remain); he was supported from our spritsail yard, which hooked in the mizen-rigging. A soldier of the 69th Regiment having broken the upper quarter-gallery window, I jumped in myself and was followed by others as fast as possible. I found the cabin doors fastened, and some Spanish officers fired their pistols; but having broken open the doors, the soldiers fired, and the Spanish brigadier (commodore with a distinguishing pennant) fell as he was retreating to the quarter-deck. I pushed onwards immediately for the quarter-deck, where I found Captain Berry in possession of the poop, and the Spanish ensign hauling down. I passed with my people and Lieutenant Pearson along the larboard gangway to the fore-castle, where I met two or three Spanish officers, prisoners to my seamen; they delivered their swords.

A fire of pistols, or muskets, opening from the admiral's stern gallery of the *San Josef*, I directed the soldiers to fire into her stern; and calling to Captain Miller, ordered him to send more men into the *San Nicolas*, and directed my people to board the first-rate, which was done in an instant, Captain Berry assisting me in the main chains. At this moment a Spanish officer looked over the quarter-deck rail, and said they surrendered. From this most welcome intelligence it was not long before I was on the quarter-deck; when the Spanish captain, with a bow, presented me his sword, and said the admiral was dying of his wounds. I asked him, on his honour, if the ship was surrendered. He declared she was, on which I gave him my hand, and desired him to call on his officers and ship's company and tell them of it, which he did, and on the quarter-deck of a Spanish first-rate, extravagant as the story may seem, did I receive the swords of the vanquished Spaniards, which, as I received, I gave to William Fearney, one of my bargemen, who put them with the greatest *sang froid* under his arm. I was surrounded by Captain Berry, Lieutenant Pearson (of the 69th), John Sykes, John Thompson, Francis Cook, all old *Agamemnons*, and several other brave men, sailors and soldiers. Thus fell these two ships."

THE BATTLE OF THE NILE, 1798.

Bonaparte had made Piedmont a French province. Rome was occupied by French troops, and the arms of France threatened all Europe. The so-called "army of England" still waited on the French coast, but while the British fleet kept the seas there was little probability of that army effecting the vaunted invasion of Britain. Therefore the "destiny" which the great general of the Republic of France set before himself was the conquest of Egypt, which, while it would compensate for the loss of the French possessions in the West Indies, would enable him to harass if not to invade British territory in the East. An army of 30,000 men, mostly composed of soldiers who had defeated the Austrians in Italy, was at Toulon, ready to sail for

Alexandria and the mouths of the Nile. The destination of this force had been kept secret from the enemies of France; and though the English blockading squadron was on the alert and watching the French coast, a continuance of contrary winds had driven our ships from those waters, so that on the 19th of May, 1798, Bonaparte had been able to put to sea with a great fleet of men-of-war and transports, and to sail up the Mediterranean.

The first important operation in the plan, which Bonaparte was to carry out under the orders of the "directory," was to besiege and capture Malta, still held by the Knights of St. John of Jerusalem, who had not acknowledged the French Republic, though there were those among them who were ready to espouse French interests. It is to the treasonable counsels of these men that the capitulation of the island, two days after Bonaparte had summoned it to surrender, is to be attributed. Hompesch, the grand master, was weak and old, and finding himself surrounded by those who betrayed instead of supporting him, he neglected to fortify and man the works at Lavalette, which could have kept the French fleet at bay till the English came to the relief of the island; for Nelson was already seeking everywhere for the enemy, who escaped his observation because he was unprovided with frigates with which to make more rapid observations.

On the 19th of June, after having plundered Malta, from which he obtained a considerable sum of money, Bonaparte re-embarked for Egypt, leaving General Vaubois and a garrison in the island. On the 29th he came to Alexandria, and landed the next day in considerable haste and confusion, for it was known that Nelson was searching the seas, and the French dreaded discovery. There was some reason for this fear, for as they sailed from the coast of Caramania to the north side of Candia they came close to the English fleet, which was only prevented from seeing them by a thick fog. It is almost amazing to reflect what a remarkable difference this fog probably made in the history of the world; for had Nelson seen and borne down upon the French, as he certainly would have done, they would have been destroyed or captured, and Bonaparte himself would most likely either have been killed or have been taken prisoner.

Nelson had gone hither and thither looking for the foe: he had returned up the Mediterranean without instructions, and with no actual knowledge of the expedition in which the French fleet was engaged.

Without light frigates to obtain information he groped his way by a sort of instinct, and having heard of the capture of Malta, made the best of his way thither, but too late; he immediately, by a shrewd guess, sailed for the mouth of the Nile, and actually arrived at Alexandria the day before it was sighted by the French. Finding no French fleet there he steered along the southern side of Candia, where he was close to the enemy without knowing it, crossed the Mediterranean, and returned to Sicily. Six hundred leagues had been sailed with incredible expedition. His ship, the old *Vanguard*, was nearly strained to pieces; but only staying to re-victual and take in water, he once more turned towards Egypt, and on the 28th of July, in the Morea, learned that the French had been seen between Candia and the Egyptian coast about four weeks previously.

It must not be supposed that the admiral had actually wasted the time which had passed without meeting the French fleet, and although he bitterly complained of the want of frigates, he continued to make the best of circumstances. The men of his crews were so constantly exercised in gunnery practice that they attained remarkable proficiency, and evening after evening he assembled his captains on board the *Vanguard*, and explained to them the different plans he had formed for attacking the enemy, varying with the different positions in which it was conceivable that he might encounter him. He took great care of his youngest officers, looking on himself in an especial degree as their instructor and guardian while they were afloat under his command. One or two of his midshipmen always breakfasted with him, and while entertaining them at his own table he put off the great commander, and entered into all their boyish jokes, and in manner and feeling seemed as gay-hearted and youthful as any of his party. The amusement of the men also was not forgotten, and when their practice in gunnery was over they were allowed to join in various games, to dance, and to sing. It would, in fact, be difficult to imagine how the men could have sustained such an arduous service but for the cheerful courage and sympathy of their commander.

Bonaparte, after landing his troops—a considerable number of whom were drowned in the haste with which they crowded on shore—took Alexandria without much difficulty, and from its walls proclaimed to Egypt that he came as the friend of the Sultan to deliver the people from the oppression of the Mamelukes, and that he and his soldiers respected the Prophet and the Koran. On the 7th of July the army moved to Cairo, marching over burning sands, from which they suffered very considerably. On the 21st, on arriving within sight of the Great Pyramids, they had to give battle to the Mameluke force under Ibrahim Bey and Murad Bey. The victory of the French was rapid and decisive, and Bonaparte entered Cairo two days afterwards without resistance, and assembled a divan of the Turkish and Arab chiefs, to whom he proposed the civil administration of the country.

But these intentions were frustrated by the destruction of the fleet which he had left at Alexandria. Nelson had crowded sail once more for the mouth of the Nile, and his fleet of thirty-seven seventy-fours, one fifty-gun ship, and a fourteen-ton brig was in sight of Alexandria on the morning of the 1st of August. At four in the afternoon Captain Hood, in the *Zealous*, signalized the enemy's fleet at anchor in Aboukir Bay, and Nelson, who had scarcely been able to eat or to sleep, at once ordered dinner to be served, and gaily prepared for action. At half-past five the signal was given to form in line, and before six o'clock they were approaching the enemy, whose force consisted of one ship of the line of one hundred and twenty guns, three of eighty guns, and nine of seventy-four, moored in compact line of battle, describing an obtuse angle, close in with the shore, while they were flanked by four frigates, gun-boats, and a battery of guns and mortars placed on an island in their van.

Nelson at once determined to take the inner side of the French line; for where a French ship could swing a British ship could anchor. As the two leading ships approached, the French opened fire, and the guns on Aboukir island also began to play upon our vessels as they rounded the shoal, though they ceased when the ships became closely engaged, as they were then likely to strike the French van. By seven o'clock eight of the British fleet had anchored and were in close action, the first of them being Nelson's flagship the *Vanguard*, which was within half-pistol shot of the *Spartiate*, the third ship in the enemy's line. The *Culloden*, commanded by Captain Trowbridge, unfortunately grounded on a ledge of rocks, whence no efforts could dislodge her, and consequently she took no part in the action. At about half-past nine eight of the French ships in the van had surrendered, and soon afterwards the *Orient*, one of their vessels, was in flames.

At about this time Nelson, who was always in a prominent position, and exposed to the fire of the enemy, received a wound in the head which caused the skin of the forehead to fall over his remaining eye, and at first both he and those around him feared that he was seriously if not fatally injured. He was on his quarter-deck scanning a rough sketch of the Bay of Aboukir, which had been found in a prize recently taken by the *Swiftsure*, when a piece of langridge shot struck him and inflicted the wound. The sudden darkness, and the extreme pain from the injury to the bone, caused him to think that the hurt was mortal, and as he fell into the arms of Captain Berry, who stood near him, he exclaimed, "I am killed; remember me to my wife." When he was carried down into the cockpit, the surgeon, who was attending to a wounded seaman, would have left his patient to attend to the admiral; but Nelson, with that unselfish fortitude which distinguished him and endeared him to the men, motioned to him to keep away, saying, "No, I will take my turn with my brave fellows." When his turn came, the wound was found to be painful but not dangerous. It was properly bound up, and he quickly reappeared on the quarter-deck, giving orders for the boats to go to the assistance of the enemy's burning vessel, many of the crew of which were saved either by the boats or by being dragged into the ports of the British vessels by our seamen. The French Admiral Brueys was already dead, and among several hundreds who perished was the brave Commodore Casa Bianca and his son, a boy of only ten years of age. Both of these were seen floating by a shattered mast when the ship blew up, with such an awful explosion, that the battle ceased, for full ten minutes not a gun being fired, until the French ship *Franklin* recommenced, to be quickly silenced. By midnight the *Tonnant* was the only vessel on the enemy's side which continued actively engaged; but her masts were shot away, and she was compelled to veer cable and take up a station in the rear.

Again the battle ceased till day broke, when four of the French ships resumed the engagement with two of the English, which were soon joined by others. The French frigate *Artemise* fired a final broadside and then struck her colours. She soon afterwards blew up, and the four French line-of-battle ships and two frigates dropped so far to leeward that they were almost out of gunshot. Two of them ran on shore and afterwards struck their colours. The two others escaped, only one of our ships, the *Zealous*, being in a position to chase them, but they were afterwards taken, with one of the frigates, by the British squadron in the Mediterranean. Eight of the thirteen French ships of the line had surrendered, two had escaped, and two were on shore with their colours flying. One of these was afterwards taken, and the other was set on fire by the crew, who escaped to shore. Thus eleven line-of-battle ships were lost to the French. The British loss in killed and wounded was 896, Westcott of the *Majestic* being the only captain who fell in the engagement. Of the French, 3105, including the wounded, were sent on shore by *cartel*, and 5225 perished.

"Victory," said Nelson, "is not a name strong enough for such a scene." He called it a conquest. The French navy was almost destroyed. The British fleet had swept the seas. The hopes of Europe to oppose the hitherto successful arms of the French were revived. Malta was blockaded, to be subsequently taken by the British, and Bonaparte, after a long struggle in Egypt, began a new scheme of conquest, after the temporary rest of the peace of Amiens, by which the war, instead of being concluded, was only postponed.

THE DEATH OF TIPPOO SULTAUN.

The pictures of scenes of English history during the middle and latter portion of the reign of George III. are almost necessarily representations of battles by sea or land, or of incidents associated with that state of war in which the nation continued for so many years. It would therefore require considerable space to describe in detail those successive military and naval operations which gave to this country such immense influence in Europe, and at the same time compelled our statesmen to lay a heavy burden of taxation upon the people. Not on the Continent only, but in India, our troops were engaged in a long-continued struggle against the enormous influence of France, stimulated by the victorious career of Bonaparte, whose ambition, but for the constant and impregnable opposition of the English, would have led him to assume the dictatorship of every country to which he could carry his successful battalions. It is certain that the serious check which he had received in Egypt had prevented Bonaparte from turning his immediate attention to India. Affairs in Paris demanded his return, and he reached the capital of France to take steps for having himself proclaimed First Consul of that republic for which he was to pronounce a new constitution before he finally converted it into an empire.

That he looked forward to the possibility of supplanting us in the East is shown by the letter which he sent to Tippoo Sultaun from Egypt, requesting him to send a confidential person to Suez or Cairo to confer with him and concert measures for "the liberation of India." It is doubtful whether the letter reached the Sultaun, but it is certain that this warlike prince, whose remorseless cruelties had already roused the indignation of many of the native chiefs as well as of the British in India, had previously made overtures to form an alliance with the French republic. In 1797 he had sent an embassy to Cabool to bring down the Afghan tribes, and had negotiated or intrigued with the Nizam of the Deccan and other native princes to help him to recover what he had lost in previous engagements with the English; and finally he sent two representatives to the Isle of France to obtain the co-operation of the French, requesting that he might have an immediate supply of troops (30,000 or 40,000 men) to expel the English from every part of Hindostan.

A few Frenchmen were sent to Seringapatam; but their arrival and the other preparations made by Tippoo were known to the government at Calcutta. The Earl of Mornington (afterwards Marquis of Wellesley), who was governor-general, determined to anticipate the movements of the Sultaun, and after demanding explanations, which were never given, sent General Harris into the Mysore country with 24,000 men, and called up General Smart with the Bombay army of about 7000 men to co-operate with Harris. The general was also joined at Vellore by a strong British detachment serving with the Nizam, and by some regiments of Sepoys which the Nizam had raised, and who fought admirably under the command of British officers. Harris entered the Mysore territory on the 5th of March, 1799, and moved straight for Seringapatam, reducing all the forts in his way. General Smart advanced with greater difficulty, for he was encountered by the main army of the Sultaun; and when on the 27th Harris was within two days' march of Seringapatam he found Tippoo already there with his troops drawn up to oppose him.

It was in this action that great distinction was first achieved by a colonel who, though then known only as a promising and able officer, afterwards became the chief military commander, not only in England, but in Europe, and was destined to break the power of Napoleon Bonaparte, and after twelve years of warfare to be instrumental in restoring peace. Colonel Arthur Wellesley commanded the 33d Regiment in the action before Seringapatam, and it was this regiment which may be said to have decided the battle; while from that time the career of Wellesley in India was an almost unbroken series of brilliant successes, to be followed by a still more remarkable series of achievements in Spain, France, and Belgium, when the English nation had unanimously appointed him as their general.

The defeat of Tippoo Sultaun, however, was followed by his retreat into the strong fortifications of Seringapatam, which was then besieged by the British from the 5th of April till the 4th of May, the numerous obstacles which prevented an approach to the walls having been overcome by General Baird and Colonel Wellesley. Then the actual siege commenced. A detachment of the Bombay army under Colonel Hunt drove the enemy from the north side of the Cauvery, and held a position in the ruins of an old redoubt and village from which they could enfilade the enemy's entrenchment on the south side of the river. On the evening of the 27th of April an attack was made on the enemy's post on the front and right of the British line, and was skilfully conducted by Colonel Wellesley, who thus kept the ground where the breaching batteries were to be placed. Tippoo made a desperate attempt to regain this post, but the troops had received orders to hold it to the last extremity and could not be dislodged. This seems to have caused the Sultaun to despond. He made no further important effort to prevent the capture of the city, but after some feeble attempt at resistance appears only to have determined to fight to the last, and to fulfil his destiny by finding a grave amidst the ruins of the stronghold.

The decisive assault was intrusted to Major-general Baird, who fifteen years before had undergone a long and cruel captivity in the fortress, under the orders of Tippoo's father Hyder Ali, and whose great courage and determination well fitted him for such a duty. He

was instructed by General Harris to capture the ramparts first, and therefore divided his force into two columns, one to move along the northern and the other along the southern rampart until both should join on the east face, thus making the whole course of the ramparts before descending on the town. To do this secretly and effectually the different corps were moved silently into the trenches during the night. The attack was to be made on the following day. There could be no delay, for the British troops were worn out with fatigue and want. During the night the English batteries kept up a heavy fire on the breach to prevent it being repaired. At one o'clock the voice of Baird was heard like a trumpet exclaiming, "Now, my brave fellows, follow me, and prove yourselves worthy of the name of British soldiers!" They rushed across the river under a heavy fire of rockets and musketry from the fort, they ascended the glacis, and reached the summit of the breach, where they planted the British colours, and then the two streams of red uniforms, like two trains of gunpowder simultaneously kindled, were seen to run along the northern and southern ramparts, bearing every obstacle before them, and planting their colours as they went, until they reached the point of reunion. On the left Tippoo was present himself, and there the enemy made a desperate resistance; but they could not withstand the determined onslaught of the English, who were infuriated by the knowledge that the barbarous chieftain had murdered the prisoners taken during the siege.

Resistance ceased when the two divisions met on the eastern rampart. The slaughter was at an end, and Seringapatam was taken; but the Sultaun was nowhere to be seen. It was reported that he had been shot and was lying dead under one of the gateways, but even his family could give no information, nor would they open the palace gates without his permission. It was necessary that there should be no doubt of Tippoo's fate, or the taking of the capital would be of comparatively little advantage. Alive or dead he must be discovered, and after some negotiations and delay, the palace officials were induced to open the palace gates that search might be made. Two princes, who had formerly been the captives of Cornwallis, aided Baird and his officers in their quest, and at a gateway on the north face of the fort, which was covered with hundreds of slain, an explornation was made by torchlight. From the heap of dead the yet warm body of Tippoo was brought out; the eyes were open, and it was thought that he was still alive, for the countenance was not distorted, but his heart had ceased to beat, and three wounds in the body and one in the temple from a musket-ball must have been fatal. His turban, jacket, and sword-belt were gone, but the body was recognized by some of his people to be that of the Sultaun. On the following day his body was interred in the grave of his father with military honours amidst a terrible storm of thunder and lightning, by which several persons, Europeans and natives, lost their lives.

Sir David Wilkie's famous picture, reproduced in our engraving, represents the scene after the discovery of the dead Sultaun. General Baird, standing in the gateway beneath which Tippoo received his fatal wounds, gives orders that the body shall be carried to the palace. The grating beneath the step on which the victorious general is standing serves to light the dungeon in which he was for nearly four years immured by Hyder Ali and his son—the same Tippoo Sultaun who now lies prostrate, bereft of his crown, his kingdom, and his life.

It is worth noting that the taking of Seringapatam gave occasion to a young artist to introduce the first truly striking work of art which had ever been exhibited in this country as a *panorama*. Robert Ker Porter was then a student in the Royal Academy, and comparatively unknown, though he afterwards obtained some distinction as Sir Robert Ker Porter, author of *Travels in Persia*, while his two sisters, Jane and Anna Maria, were among the best known writers of fiction in their day. When Seringapatam was taken Porter was a mere lad, and with remarkable ability and enthusiasm he at once began to cover a canvas 200 feet long with the successive scenes which accompanied the capture of the great fortress. In six weeks he had completed the work, and Benjamin West, who was then president of the Royal Academy, obtained an early view of the picture, and pronounced it to be a miracle of precocious talent. When it was arranged for exhibition, vast numbers of persons of all classes flocked to see it, and among them Dr. Dibdin, who says: " I can never forget its first impression on my own mind. It was as a thing dropped from the clouds, —all fire, energy, intelligence, and animation. You looked a second time, the figures moved and were commingled in hot and bloody fight. You saw the flash of the cannon, the glitter of the bayonet, and the gleam of the falchion. You longed to be leaping from crag to crag with Sir David Baird, who is hallooing his men on to victory. Then again you seemed to be listening to the groans of the dying—and more than one female was carried out swooning." Unfortunately this picture was destroyed by fire, but engravings of it were made by Vendramini.

THE "PRESS-GANG."

It is easy to understand that during a long period of successive wars by land and sea, it became necessary to use constant efforts to find able recruits for the army and to man the navy with efficient seamen. The recruiting-officer and his party were frequently at every town and important village in the kingdom, and all sorts of inducements were offered to young fellows to enlist, while those who were not easily persuaded were frequently made drunk and cajoled into taking the bounty-money, after which they were quickly marched off in company with others to the nearest military depôt.

While the army was thus increased for foreign wars, public security in London and other towns was little improved. Highway robbery and crimes of violence were of constant occurrence, and only a few patrols and watchmen were appointed to guard the streets. In 1763 the numerous roads near London were protected by no greater force than a patrol of eighty mounted constables, and in the metropolis itself prisoners were frequently rescued from the lock-up houses. It may be believed that as a system of rewards for the capture of thieves was instituted, there was often great confusion and injustice in the accusation and arrest of alleged ill-doers, and as hanging was the penalty even for comparatively small offences, condemned criminals of not very atrocious character could be found to purchase their lives or liberties by enlisting for military service in "the Indies." That this system introduced among the recruits a number of atrocious ruffians there can be little doubt, and the scenes on board the "tenders," to which military and naval recruits were shipped, were of the most dreadful and revolting description. In almost every street, especially by the waterside, crimps lay in wait to entice likely-looking fellows into houses where they were locked up and regularly entrapped, at the same time they were drugged with strong drink, or, if they were too violent in their resistance, were knocked on the head and left till it was time to take them off by the river. Men were even "arrested for debt" by gangs of fellows, who took this method of kidnapping them and carried them off without giving them the opportunity of proving the falsity of the charge.

The method of manning the navy was immeasurably worse, for men were kidnapped according to law by the press-gangs, or armed bands of ruffianly sailors, who seized and carried off any able-bodied fellow they could lay their hands on. Their operations were chiefly carried on in neighbourhoods not far from the river, and though they sometimes met with resistance they were usually successful in making a haul of "pressed men," for they were armed with pistols and cutlasses and did not scruple to use them. The allusions to the press-gang in the writings of Smollett and other authors at the time, show how utterly unscrupulous were the means taken to obtain hands for the navy, and how horrible were the scenes that awaited the unfortunate landsman, who was often stunned, flung neck and heels into a boat, and taken on board the tender, where any attempt at resistance was quickly and brutally repressed.

Of course the larger number of these enforced recruits was taken from the rough part of the population, from wharf and dock hands, market porters and labourers; but men of a better class were frequently pressed, especially as they could be kidnapped more easily, while the rougher sort frequently combined for their own protection, and, armed with hard and knotted bludgeons, were occasionally a match for the press-gangs, especially as, after a quick and determined defence, they could escape by the tortuous streets, where if the sailors followed them and became separated they could often make terrible reprisals.

It is remarkable that both as volunteers and pressed men the descendants of the French Protestants, who had settled about Spitalfields and in some other parts of London, were frequently to be found in the royal navy. Strange that, as at the battle of the Boyne the Huguenot contingent had fought so fiercely against the regiments of their countrymen, the children of later refugees were

among the most active opponents of the French at sea. France paid dearly for the persecution of the Protestants, who became denationalized when they found protection and a home in England.

Many strange and pathetic stories could have been told of the havoc made in poor families by the press-gang, both among the Spitalfields weavers and others of the working-classes. Men had even been known to cripple themselves in order that they might not be seized and torn from their wives and children; while others learned to simulate lameness or idiocy, or even went about dressed in women's clothes, in fear of being pressed and sent abroad without the least opportunity of remonstrance. Many, however, were taken, and returned to tell the story. One man, a weaver, went out on a Saturday night to fetch what was then, and still is, a favourite supper of hot baked sheep's head for himself and his wife. He had scarcely left his own street-door before he was pinioned, gagged, and taken off to Tower stairs, whence he was sent to sea. He remained for three years on foreign service without having had any opportunity of communicating with his wife, though she may possibly have heard of him through some friend. She was an industrious and helpful woman, and as she could earn her own living as a clear-starcher, remained living in the same place, and waited until hope nearly failed, and she had given up her husband as killed or lost, when on a Saturday night she heard a quick foot upon the stair, and in another moment a bronzed, bearded man (whom she knew by his voice, in spite of the change that three years of sea-service had wrought in him) called out, "Well, Betty, I've brought the sheep's head at last, but I've been a good while gone for it," and actually put a smoking supper upon the table. He had heard that she was alive and had lived in the same house, waiting for his return, and when his ship was paid off, had, with a queer touch of humour, contrived to get home on a Saturday night, and to take with him the dainty that had been expected three years before.

More sad and tragical stories were told however—stories of young men captured and taken from the sides of their sweethearts at country wakes and fairs, of athletic young Thames watermen—who if they were freemen were supposed to be exempt—kidnapped, and then left without the chance of making any appeal that would be likely to find sympathetic listeners. One tale of a fine young fellow, who in spite of remonstrance was surrounded by a remorseless gang, and forcibly taken from the side of his young and pretty bride on their wedding-day, is among the annals of this fearful time.

But for the tremendous exigencies of the war, and the turbulent condition of society, in which individual wrongs inflicted by the government for the purpose of increasing the fighting power of the country were regarded only as necessary evils, the brutalities of the recruiting parties would have been sufficient to cause an insurrection. As it was, considerable improvements had to be made in the provision for the navy, and unless the crews were actually engaged in war or on a voyage looking for the enemy there was mostly a mutinous disposition, as might have been expected among men who were forced into the service. Yet these were among the heroes who made the English fleet feared all over the world. When it came to fighting, the pressed men let loose their patriotism, and forgot their personal wrongs in the honour of the country and their determination not to be beaten. Nor were there wanting numerous instances of men, who, having been first pressed, became voluntary sailors, adopting as a chosen profession that to which they had at first manifested considerable repugnance.

THE DEFENCE OF SARAGOSSA.

Even in an extended history it would be difficult to give a detailed account of the various engagements in which Britain was called upon to check the arrogant assumptions of France during the early part of the present century. All that can be done in these pages is to indicate some of the more remarkable episodes of those tremendous conflicts in which the arms of England were conspicuous, and amidst the pictures which more immediately arrest our attention that of the "Maid of Saragossa" is one of the most prominent.

The siege of Saragossa, however, had been raised before the entry of British troops into Spain, and even before Admiral Collingwood went to Gibraltar, and thence proceeded to Cadiz to take command of the fleet that had assembled there. Indeed it was only when Spain had risen against the French usurpers, and had begun to succeed in a determined effort to break the yoke imposed upon her by Bonaparte, that England, instead of being her enemy, became her ally. On the 4th of June, the birthday of George III., a proclamation was issued that his majesty, having taken into consideration the glorious resolution of the Spaniards to deliver their country from the tyranny and usurpation of France, and the assurances his majesty had received from several of the provinces of Spain of their friendly disposition towards England, he was pleased to order that all hostilities against Spain should immediately cease. Bonaparte had thrust his elder brother Joseph on the throne of Spain, had overrun the country with French armies, and had taken possession of the principal fortresses. All seemed to be confusion, and though the patriots had formed into considerable bodies in various parts of the kingdom, they were destitute of competent leaders, and while the defence was sustained by insurrection, the mode of warfare consisted chiefly of irregular attacks by bodies of peasantry, outlaws, and stragglers from the more regular army, who formed into "guerilla" troops, and carried on a contest which, though it obtained few great successes, harassed and perplexed the invading forces, who were at first scattered over a wide extent of country.

On entering Catalonia the French troops under Duhesme became involved in a war which was waged by the peasantry and the mountaineers; and on the 22d of July General Dupont, who had endeavoured to penetrate into Andalusia, and who had been completely surrounded and defeated in several combats by the Andalusian army of Castaños, and by large bodies of armed peasants, was compelled to lay down his arms. Above 18,000 were thus made prisoners, and the artillery and baggage were also taken. The French troops were thoroughly beaten, and when the news reached Madrid great was the consternation of the king, Joseph Bonaparte, who, having been obtruded to his new throne only a fortnight before, at once called a council of war, which advised immediate retirement to Vittoria, a city lying conveniently near to the French frontier. The retreat of the French from Madrid began on the 1st of August, but the Spanish General Castaños did not enter until the 23d.

One of the immediate results of the defeat of the French in Andalusia and the evacuation of Madrid, was the raising of the siege of Saragossa. The people of this city were distinguished by unyielding bravery, which, although the place was badly fortified, enabled them to withstand the assault of a considerable French army which had invested and bombarded it, until the outworks and half of the city itself were taken. The people had chosen Palafox as their commander, and it was he who was summoned to surrender in the following laconic message, sent by Verdier, the French general. " Head-quarters, Santa Engracia: Capitulation." His answer was equally brief, and to the purpose. " Head-quarters, Saragossa: War to the knife." (*Guerra al Cuchillo.*) Palafox summoned a council of war, and it was determined to defend the remaining portion of the city inch by inch; to retire in case of defeat across the Ebro, and to destroy the bridge after passing the river. The same night the French were attacked by Palafox and the Spaniards with irresistible fury, and after eleven days, during which Verdier could not hold his position—and his decision was hastened by tidings from Madrid of the disasters in Andalusia and the retirement of Joseph Bonaparte—the siege was raised.

So important was Saragossa as a position, however, that in November, 1808, a large army under Marshals Moncey and Mortier again invested it, in spite of the desperate valour of Palafox, who had, perhaps imprudently, sallied out against the foe, and been twice defeated, first at Tuleda, and again under the walls of the city. The outworks were carried, and the French began a furious bombardment amidst repeated combats. The besiegers could not estimate the desperate valour of the people against whom they were fighting, for not only men but women took part in the defence, and foremost among the latter was a young, and as report says fair, maiden belonging to the labouring class of the country. Known by her name of Augustina, she was afterwards recognized throughout Europe as "the maid of Saragossa," and is so called in history, which has preserved a record of her courage and devotion. For she and her band of heroic women served on the batteries amidst that scene of carnage and of fire; and when at length, on the 27th of January, 1809, a general assault was made, and the French at last penetrated into the city, she and her followers continued to aid in that desperate resistance, by which even old men and children endeavoured to contest the progress

of the enemy, not only house by house, but room by room, so that the very dwellings were fought for, taken and retaken, as desperately as though each had been a separate fortress. Amidst the flame and bloodshed the maid of Saragossa was a prominent figure, and her valour was an illustration of the resolution that animated the whole population.[1]

An outbreak of fever and the losses they had sustained in the conflict led the inhabitants and their commanders at last to listen to terms of honourable capitulation; but by that time the war in Spain was about to assume an entirely new aspect, for British bayonets were already glittering on the shores of the Peninsula, and Sir Arthur Wellesley was about to commence a career which did not end till European politics had undergone a change, and a new era of English history had been inaugurated.

THE BATTLE OF WATERLOO.

It is neither noble nor wise to lay too much stress on the observance of the anniversaries of great victories, and even boastful allusion to such warlike successes as may at the time have been fit subjects for national rejoicing, is a custom "more honoured in the breach than the observance." We live in times when the great battle on the field of Waterloo,—though it need not, and in truth cannot, be forgotten, and may well be remembered by all those who were engaged in it as an historical event fraught with enormous interest to succeeding generations,—must no more be regarded with a revival of hostile feelings, or with mean-souled triumph, than other battles which have passed out of the region of strife, and should be looked at as we look at old historical pictures portraying events that mark the struggles which precede the fusion of races, or the conflicts that prepare for the lasting amity of nations.

---

[1] In our illustration, Augustina, "The Maid of Saragossa," has the match in her hand ready to discharge the gun, of which the commander Palafox and Father Consolacion direct the pointing.

It may be remarked that the Duke of Wellington until his death continued to celebrate the anniversary of "Waterloo" by a dinner at Apsley House: but what a celebration it was! As years went on there was little in it that could be called jubilant, even if that element had ever had a place in the observance. Round the table of the great commander were gathered his old comrades-in-arms, not to vaunt of their deeds, or to indulge in defiant toasts and boastful congratulations, but to meet each other—a company becoming smaller and smaller as the years went by—and to contrast, perhaps frequently with grateful hearts, the growing sentiments of peace with a great nation which had passed through fierce and fiery vicissitudes, and the long wars that had drained both England and France of noble blood, of brave men, and of treasure that might have been used to make the world better by the example of the leading powers of Europe. The evil time has passed, and we no longer celebrate the great victory. We have even learned to speak of it with some regard and with sincere respect for those who were the vanquished; while, if the French have not entirely forgiven us for the foremost part we played in breaking up the power of what threatened to be a wide-spreading empire, they have most of them learned to be glad that they were delivered from an ambition that would have led France captive, and kept her in chains in the name of glory.

There seems to be little reason to believe that the orders given by the Duke of Wellington to his officers, before the march to Waterloo, were hastily communicated in consequence of sudden intelligence received at a ball given by the Duchess of Richmond at Brussels. Byron's famous lines have perhaps been chiefly instrumental in perpetuating what was a mere report, and it was of course regarded as a romantic incident in the first incomplete rumours of the event; but detractors of the great general endeavoured to prove from his presence at the ball, that he was altogether unprepared for the tactics of his opponents. Even if this had been the case, it must have been consummate skill which could at once have made such dispositions as contributed to so decided a victory; but as a matter of fact the report was without foundation.

It was on the 11th of June that Bonaparte quitted Paris to open the campaign, saying, "Je vais me mésurer avec ce Villainton;" and on the 15th of June he crossed the frontier. The duke's head-quarters were at Brussels. On his left lay Marshal Blücher with the Prussian army, whose head-quarters were at Namur. The question was, by what roads will Bonaparte advance? His army was conducted by Ney, Soult, and Grouchy, three experienced generals acting under his directions, and while the British and Prussian forces were necessarily far apart, the French might approach by either of four great high-roads or by one of the numerous bye-roads.

It was the intention of Bonaparte to commence by taking the Prussians by surprise, and if he failed to overpower them, at least to separate them from the British, and then to overwhelm the latter with his entire force. On the 15th of June, at two or three o'clock in the morning, the foremost columns began their march, and at dawn they had driven in the Prussian outposts. By the afternoon they had divided into four bodies and crossed the Sambre, where Ziethen, who commanded the advanced guard, was compelled to retire, but retreated fighting step by step, so that the main army, under Blucher, might have time to concentrate on the Sombref, where the forces afterwards occupied the villages of St. Armand and Ligny, while Bonaparte's head-quarters were established at Charleroi.

Early in the preliminary skirmishing Ney was detached by the emperor with his left column of 45,000 men to continue his march along the road leading from Charleroi to Brussels, to advance upon Quatre Bras, and to separate the communication between Wellington and Blucher. This Quatre Bras was a farm-house occupying the point of junction of the roads from Charleroi to Brussels, and from Nivelles to Namur. Prince Bernard of Saxe-Weimar, commanding a brigade of Netherlanders, was stationed at Frasné, and there intercepted the march of Ney, who drove him back by the force of superior numbers; but the prince retreated upon Quatre Bras, the point to which Ney's efforts were directed, and there having fortified the farm-house, determined to make a stand, having been reinforced by the Prince of Orange, who brought his troops to his aid.

These events rapidly succeeded each other on the 15th of June, and the Duke of Wellington, so far from being unacquainted with the threatened danger, was only waiting to learn upon which quarter the enemy intended to commence the attack. On the first intelligence that the Prussian outposts were driven in, he issued orders that the army might be ready. It was not till he heard that the French troops were being massed in the valley of the Sambre that he knew the attack was to be made on Charleroi, and when this was ascertained he issued orders, from his hotel at Brussels, for the British troops to commence their march.

This was quietly done at five o'clock in the afternoon, and as it was then necessary to wait for some hours till the orders could be distributed through the various corps, and as it was probably important to avoid the inevitable excitement and alarm which would be caused in the city by a sudden demonstration, he went with a number of his officers, to keep an engagement, to be present at a ball given by the Duchess of Richmond. It was a brilliant assembly, and of course the guests were unconscious of the tremendous events which were so imminent. The "Iron Duke" preserved his usual equanimity, and it was only at about midnight, when the enjoyment of the splendid festival was at its height, that the word was quietly passed, first to the general officers and afterwards to the subordinates. Without confusion or excitement, and also without much of leave-taking, the officers left by twos and threes, to take their places at the head of their musters, so that they might be in readiness to march to the field of the great battle that was to be fought on the 18th. This then was the occurrence of which so much was made by the detractors of the great general, and to which such a romantic interest was not unnaturally attached by those who saw a picture of the scene in the lines of the poet, whose verses were eagerly read and quoted, though they were but an imaginary account of the event:—

> "There was a sound of revelry by night,
>   And Belgium's capital had gathered then
> Her beauty, and her chivalry; and bright
>   The lamps shone o'er fair women and brave men;
> A thousand hearts beat happily, and when
>   Music arose with its voluptuous swell,
> Soft eyes looked love to eyes which spake again,
>   And all went merry as a marriage-bell:
> But hush! hark! a deep sound strikes like a rising knell!
> * * * * * * * * * * *
> Ah! then and there was hurrying to and fro,
>   And gathering tears, and tremblings of distress,
> And cheeks all pale, which but an hour ago
>   Blush'd at the praise of their own loveliness;
> And there were sudden partings, such as press
>   The life from out young hearts, and choking sighs
> Which ne'er might be repeated: who would guess
>   If ever more should meet those mutual eyes,
> Since upon night so sweet such awful morn could rise!

> And there was mounting in hot haste; the steed,
> The mustering squadron, and the clattering car,
> Went pouring forward with impetuous speed,
> And swiftly forming in the ranks of war;
> And the deep thunder, peal on peal afar;
> And near, the beat of the alarming drum
> Roused up the soldier ere the morning star;
> While throng'd the citizens with terror dumb,
> Or whispering with white lips—'The foe! they come! they come!'"[1]

The narrative of the great battle is an oft-told tale, and the mere outline of some of its more prominent features is still sufficient to recall to the imagination of many readers the picture of the whole tremendous scene which was enacted during that wild and stormy Sunday. The position of the British army at Waterloo had already been agreed upon between Wellington and Blucher, in the event of the Prussians being compelled to retreat from Ligny. The English troops, reinforced by the Brunswickers, had held Quatre Bras, the farmhouse at the four roads, where the fight was again and again resumed amidst fire and smoke, in the ineffectual attempts of the enemy to carry the position. At Ligny Blucher's retreat was slow and steady, for the old "Marshal Forwards," as he was called, would only retire fighting, and contested every inch of the ground. The British who had held Quatre Bras then left it on the night of the 17th to join the main body at Waterloo, and on their way the heavy household cavalry, under Lord Uxbridge, charged and rode down a force of French cavalry which had left Ligny and endeavoured to oppose them. On the same day and during the night the junction was made between the troops of Ney and those that had been at Ligny with Napoleon Bonaparte.

It was a night of violent storm and rain, and most of our men had no place to sleep but on the miry ground or amidst the drenched cornfields. When the morning dawned the scene was dull and drear; for though the storm had ceased, the sky was overcast with clouds, through which the sun rarely broke. The position which Wellington had taken up was in front of the village of Waterloo, and crossed the high roads from Charleroi and Nivelles; it had its right thrown back to a ravine near Merke Braine, which was occupied, and its left extended to a height above the hamlet of Ter-la-Haye, which was likewise occupied; and in front of the right centre and near the Nivelles road our troops held the house and gardens of Hougoumont, and in

---

[1] Byron. *Childe Harold's Pilgrimage*, canto iii.

front of the left centre the farm of La Haye Sainte. In the rear of the British centre was the farm of Mont St. Jean, and a little further back stood the village of that name. Behind the British position was the famous old forest of Soignies. The duke's force was 72,720 men, of whom 36,273 were British, 7447 Hanoverians, 8000 Brunswickers, and 21,000 Belgians and Nassau troops.

Napoleon had occupied a range of heights in front of the British position, and not more than a mile from it; his right being in advance of Planchenois, his line crossing the Charleroi road at the farm of La Belle Alliance, his left resting on the Genappe road. Behind the French the ground rose considerably, and was skirted by thick woods. His forces must have amounted to 75,000 men, and their order of battle was grand, simple, and effective.

With sound of bugle, cheers, and warlike pomp and show, the troops moved into action, and the two armies prepared for that tremendous conflict which was to decide the fate of Europe. At a little after ten o'clock a perceptible stir along the French lines showed that an attack was about to be made, and at eleven began that tremendous assault upon Hougoumont by 30,000 men under the command of Ney. Again and again the French were repulsed, and again the awful conflict, accompanied by a tremendous cannonade, was renewed, till, amidst the flames of the corn-ricks, the farmhouse, and the out-buildings, the French were driven out. Similar attempts were then made on La Haye Sainte, which was afterwards carried by the enormous masses of troops. But Napoleon could not succeed in following up his successes by crushing the British infantry with repeated charges of cavalry. The cuirassiers, sent to cut the British army in sunder, fell beneath the close fire of those unshaken squares, in which every gap was filled as soon as it was made. The cavalry attack became a retreat, and whole squadrons were hurled against that close hedge of steel without breaking it, though the veterans of France, the light, long-armed, Polish lancers, and the armoured horsemen of the heavy cavalry stayed amidst the incessant fire that thinned their ranks, walking their horses up and down in the effort to find a break by which they might cleave their way through this wall of men.

At length came the word of command, and the British cavalry, who had as yet done little except in the few brilliant charges to relieve the defenders of the position, were called into action. The heavy brigade,

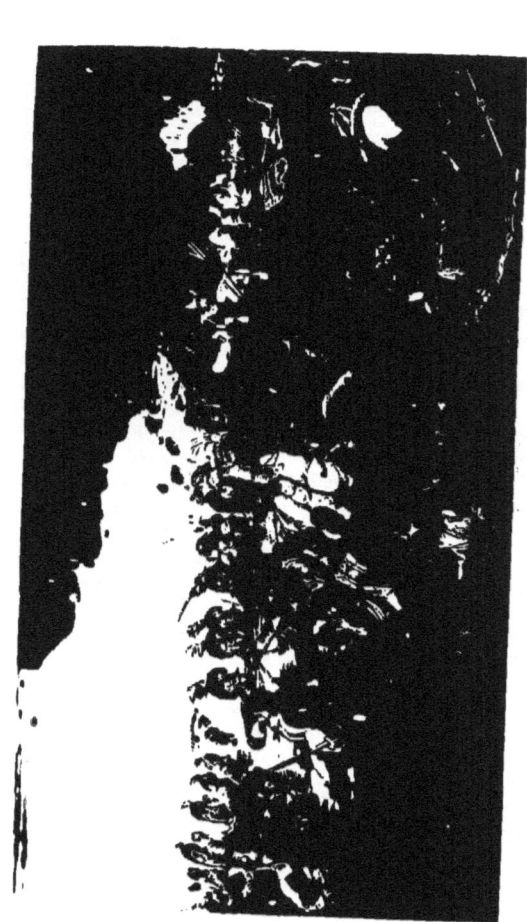

consisting of the Life Guards, the Royal Horse Guards, and the 1st Dragoons, under Lord Edward Somerset, went thundering forward upon the French, and with irresistible strength, weight, and impetuosity, swept down light troopers and steel-clad cuirassiers in one terrible onslaught, leaving none on the field but the wounded and the dead and the 2000 prisoners whom the brigade brought back with them after the decisive charge.

The battle still raged, but the British still held their ground with some of their reserves not yet called into action. The Prussians were advancing, and it was necessary to make one more decided attack on the left centre of Wellington's army near the already devastated position of La Haye Sainte. The old Imperial Guard, the veterans who had so often been regarded as almost invincible, were called up and led by Napoleon in person as far as a hollow between La Belle Alliance and the point of attack,—a hollow sheltered from the British artillery. Then Ney led them into action through a fire that thinned their ranks, while the British were protected from the return fire that covered the advance by the low range of hills behind which they were ordered to lie down till the word of command was given. In two massive columns the French veterans went on till they were approaching the British position, when the duke gave the signal through his aide-de-camp. The enemy was suddenly confronted by General Maitland's brigade of guards, and by General Adam's brigade, who rapidly moved over the brow of the hill, where they were formed five deep by the duke in person and flanked with artillery. One tremendous volley staggered the Imperial Guards of the French army, who were not easily broken, and in a moment recovered themselves and went on; but when they were within fifty yards, and in the act of deploying, another volley was poured in among them, and before they could form again, the heavy united charge of the English guards threw them together, and drove them in confusion down the hill irretrievably broken and ruined.

Napoleon, sitting on his horse, still as a statue, broke out with the bitter cry, "They are mixed, they are mixed;" and almost immediately afterwards Bulow's cannons were heard, the Prussian ranks were seen advancing, and Wellington, moving forward with his whole line of infantry supported by the cavalry and artillery, bore down upon the shattered ranks of his opponents, and the battle was over. The French army was utterly defeated, and in its retreat was pursued by the Prussians, who so completely disorganized it, that it was useless to make any further attempt to bring it again into action. In these three terrible days it had lost 30,000 men, and its leader, who had brought all Europe into coalition against his assumptions, was the first messenger who took back the news of defeat to Paris.

GEORGE THE FOURTH.

During the time of the regency and until the end of the reign of George IV., the country was almost continually in a state of political excitement, which occasionally rose to serious rioting. The social questions which were allied to demands for a wider representation of the people in parliament gave persistency to a general feeling of dissatisfaction, not only among the lower orders of society, but in many cases among the more intelligent and educated classes. It cannot be said that the character or rather the conduct of George IV. was such as to diminish these ebullitions of popular feeling. Though his manners were mostly courteous and conciliatory, and he had too much common sense to try to exercise the dogged authority and to display the obstinate opposition that had been at one time conspicuous in the relation of George III. to his ministers and to the nation, he never succeeded in obtaining the respect which had always been manifested for the domestic virtues and simplicity of life that had distinguished his father. The career of what was then called gallantry, which was scarcely resented while he was Prince of Wales and before he became regent, assumed a different aspect when he was virtually the ruler of the nation, and carried on extravagant debaucheries, to pay for which out of the revenue repeated demands were made to parliament. After numerous disreputable amours, he became associated with Mrs. Fitzherbert, to whom (though it was strenuously denied at the time) we now know that he had gone through the ceremony of marriage, and for her sake he had at one time declared that he would renounce his succession to the throne and retire from the country. The alliance that he afterwards contracted with his cousin Caroline of Brunswick resulted in a trial, the details of which, in the evidence brought against the unhappy queen, had to be excluded from decent households, and amazed and disgusted every court in Europe.

It would be to the last degree unedifying to inquire into the grounds of the charges against Caroline; but it may be said that from the very first it was remarked that her manner was characterized by a kind of indelicate levity, which some persons actually attributed to aberration of intellect. On the succession of George to the throne he determined to exclude her from claiming to be royal consort, and a bill was brought against her in the House of Lords, so that a judicial proceeding took the form of legislative enactment; but she was defended with extraordinary ability, especially by Henry Brougham, whose great talents were first recognized during this trial, to which the young advocate devoted all his vast powers of argument and rhetoric. On the first reading of the bill it obtained a considerable majority, on the second a smaller one, and on the third (taken on the 10th of November, 1820) the numbers were 108 to 99, so small a difference that it was hopeless to expect it to pass the commons. It was therefore abandoned amid great popular rejoicings throughout the country, some of the chief towns being illuminated.

At the time that George Augustus Frederick, Prince of Wales, was appointed regent, he was less disliked than distrusted, for though he was but twenty-six years old he had long before scandalized the nation, and it was feared that the orgies of Carlton House would be transferred to the royal palace. He married Caroline Amelia Elizabeth of Brunswick, for the sake of the political alliance, to which he was urged as a means of securing fresh advances from parliament for the payment of his debts. The people were unwilling to believe the alleged reasons for his subsequent separation from his wife, and the ultimate charges brought against her, because of his own disreputable conduct. So large a section of the nation espoused her cause, that during the long and harassing trial, and the repeated attacks upon her character by which it was sustained, she was regarded as a martyr to an endeavour to exclude her from the throne, to share which she had come from abroad, where she had been living after the separation which took place almost immediately after her marriage, and even before the birth of the Princess Charlotte in 1796.

After his defeat in the attempt to pass the bill against the queen, the next step of the king was to prorogue the parliament, and the claim of the queen to be crowned was still denied. The evidence given at the trial caused enthusiasm on her behalf to abate, and though she endeavoured to gain admission to Westminster Abbey on the day of the coronation, on the 19th of July, 1821, her conduct was so strangely violent that she was prevented from entering the doors. It was of course never intended that she should be admitted, and after wandering about for a time in the vain search for another entrance, she retired amidst the mingled cheers and hisses, the applause and the abuse, of the multitude which had assembled outside. Her humiliation, her prostration, was complete. She did not long survive it. On the 7th of August she lay dead at Brandenburg House, having directed that her only epitaph should be, "Here lies Caroline of Brunswick, the injured Queen of England." She was to be buried at Brandenburg, and it was necessary to remove her body to Harwich. The mob, having determined that the coffin should be borne through the midst of London, barricaded the side streets, and a serious riot ensued. The people had supported her cause against the king, from sympathy with her sorrows, respect for her family and lineage, and a deep sense of injustice that such charges should be brought against her by a husband who was notorious for profligacy, and was even at that time living an openly immoral life. The public resentment against the king, however, seemed to take the form of a scornful indifference.

At the time of the queen's death George was on a royal progress, to which he had been advised as a remedy for his unpopularity. His journey was first to Ireland, where an obelisk was erected on the spot where he landed, and the following year he went to Edinburgh, where he was received with remarkable enthusiasm by a vast concourse of people from most of the towns in Scotland, who had crowded to the capital to see and welcome him. This was really the last important public event in which he was personally concerned; but there were already great changes in the political as well as in the social aspect of the country; and at his death, on the 26th of June, 1830, his brother, William Henry, Duke of Clarence, succeeded to the throne;

and as he was a good-humoured, easy-going man, with the reputation of having popular and liberal tendencies, and his queen, Adelaide, was a charitable and amiable woman, respected and esteemed by the nation, he was borne on the tide of those great social and political reforms from which he derived a large amount of public credit, though he personally did very little to promote them, except by sometimes refraining from opposition, and from undue interference in the course of events.

The lampoons and gross satires with which George was assailed both as regent and as king show not only the dislike and the contempt in which he was held, but the habitual license with which both public acts and private reputations were assailed. Fines and imprisonment were in many instances inflicted on the libellers of majesty; but as usual, those who were punished most severely were not those who were guilty of the coarsest invective. Examples were made, not of those who most unsparingly abused the king, but among persons whose expressions had political weight because of their literary or social ability, and were therefore regarded as most dangerous to the royal authority and to its supporters in the government. The prosecution of John and Leigh Hunt for libel, for instance, was scarcely believed to have been the penalty for referring to "the first gentleman of Europe" as "a fat Adonis of fifty;" but the articles in the *Examiner* were such dangerous contributions to the tenets of the growing liberal party, that the fine and imprisonment of their author were determined on, though, as it afterwards turned out, these punishments did as much for the liberal cause as a hundred articles might have effected.

The articles in the *Examiner* and other papers of that period, however, bore little resemblance to the coarse and almost revolting vituperation which had characterized much of the political literature of the latter part of the reign of George III. and the period of the regency. The prevailing immorality of that time, the indecency of female attire, the grossness which pervaded many of the habits of society, had survived some other shameless disorders that preceded and accompanied the French revolution. The atmosphere of aristocracy appeared to be tainted with the disgusting orgies of men and the immodesty of women who were too apt to share the dissipations and encourage the debaucheries of a prince, who, having been placed under strict governance in his early youth, broke through even the common decencies of his rank and station when he escaped from control and was exposed to the allurements of vicious companions and the machinations of rival political parties.

The fierce and bitter lampoons which appeared in the earlier days before the regency seem, however, to have been emulated by later writers. It is with a kind of shudder that we now read Byron's scathing lines: "On the Occasion of His Royal Highness the Prince Regent being seen standing between the Coffins of Henry VIII. and Charles I. in the Royal Vault at Windsor:"—

> "Famed for contemptuous breach of sacred ties,
> By headless Charles see heartless Harry lies;
> Between them stands another sceptred thing,
> It moves, it reigns, in all but name, a king:
> Charles to his people, Henry to his wife,—
> In him the double tyrant starts to life;
> Justice and death have mix'd their dust in vain,
> Each royal vampire wakes to life again.
> Ah! what can tombs avail, since these disgorge
> The blood and dust of both to make a George?"

The very coarseness of invective in these words detract from what merit there is in the verse, and it cannot be regarded as worthy of the poet's genius; but it is wonderfully illustrative of the unmitigated detestation which was frequently expressed for the regent.

The extreme frugality of George III. and Queen Charlotte in private life, and the meanness which often characterized their dealings, had already become subjects of popular satire, and contrasted strongly with the reckless extravagance of the Prince of Wales. This became still more generally a subject of conversation, when, in the session of 1786, an application was made to the House of Commons for a large sum of money to clear off the king's debts, which, in spite of the enormous civil list, he had lately incurred. As there was no visible outlet by which so much money could have disappeared, people soon made a variety of surmises to account for King George's heavy expenditure: some said that the money was spent privately in corrupting Englishmen to pave the way to arbitrary power; and most people believed that their monarch was making large savings out of the public money and hoarding them up either here or at Hanover.

With the tradition of the family feuds which seemed inseparable from the royal house, the prince was on very bad terms with the king his father, and more especially with the queen. They disliked him because he was profligate, they disliked his politics, and they disliked him still more because he took for his companions the very men towards whom King George nourished the greatest aversion. In 1783, when the coalition ministry was in power and the prince had just come of age, the ministers proposed that he should have a settlement of a hundred thousand a year; but the king insisted on allowing him no more than fifty thousand, making him dependent on his bounty for the surplus. From this moment the prince became the inseparable friend and companion of Charles Fox, and among his principal associates were Sheridan and Lord North. The king and queen were further irritated by the report of the prince's private marriage, which, of course, could not be a legal one, with Mrs. Fitzherbert. As might be expected, the prince was rapidly involving himself in debt, and his difficulties had become so great in the summer of 1786 that he found it necessary to apply to the king for assistance; but he met with a peremptory refusal. In his distress the Duke of Orleans (proverbial for his immense riches and for his dissipation), who had been in England as Duke of Chartres in 1783 and 1784, and had then formed a close intimacy with the Prince of Wales, and who was now again on a visit to this country, offered his assistance, and the prince seems only to have been prevented by the earnest expostulations of his private friends from borrowing a large sum of money from the French prince.

When he found that no assistance was to be expected from the king he determined to make a show of magnanimity, and adopted the resolution of suppressing his household establishment, and retiring into a life of strict economy. The works at Carlton House were stopped, the state apartments shut up, and his race-horses, hunters, and even his coach-horses were sold by public auction. He at the same time vested £40,000 a year—the greater part of his income—for the payment of his debts. The prince's friends, and a large portion even of the populace—for in spite of his irregularities the prince was at this time far from unpopular—trumpeted him forth as the model of honesty and noble self-denial. But the king was highly displeased, and the prince's conduct was represented at court as a mere peevish exhibition of spleen, and as an attempt to make the king and his ministers unpopular. The press—that portion of it which was under government influence—published forth the prince's failings in an indecent manner; his riotous life, his relation to Mrs. Fitzherbert, and all his promiscuous amours were commented on and represented in not very decorous prints and caricatures, which again were imitated in others of a far more vulgar character.[1] This was certainly not the way to work a reformation in a young man who had already entered on a career of debauchery, and who soon exhibited a reckless disregard to reputation.

But the French revolution was approaching, and during the period when thrones were in danger the satirists and caricaturists mostly turned from the Prince of Wales against the king and queen, whose avarice and homely economics were abused with unsparing virulence that surprises modern readers. It was not till after the Prince of Wales had become regent, and had changed his political but not his social conduct, that the full tide of invective again assailed him.

THE BOMBARDMENT OF ALGIERS.

The peace which followed the defeat of Napoleon Bonaparte was concluded by a congress of the great sovereign powers and the formation of what was afterwards called the Holy Alliance,—a kind of treaty or compact, originally suggested to Alexander, Czar of Russia, by the Baroness de Krudener, afterwards adopted by Austria, Russia, and Prussia, and subsequently endorsed by most of the other European rulers. It was, of course, desired that England should join in this religious association; but the forms of government in this country forbade (and happily forbade) subscription to a compact which, however it may have professed to provide for the government of Europe by the precepts of justice, Christian charity, and peace, was soon disregarded, or was subjected to any interpretation that its promoters and supporters chose to place upon it, even before it was suffered to fall into abeyance for the purpose of suppressing popular rights and interfering with civil and religious liberty.

The Prince Regent, afterwards George IV., was practically the

[1] *The Caricature History of the Georges,* by Thomas Wright, F.S.A.

sovereign of England, for George III. had fallen into that condition of imbecility from which he never emerged until his death, on the 29th of January, 1820, in the eighty-second year of his age, and after fifty years of actual and ten of nominal sovereignty. At the close of the war Britain, upon whom the chief burden of the tremendous conflict had fallen, and who had expended nearly £200,000,000 during the last three years in sustaining it, asked and obtained nothing but what belonged to her already, or which she might have secured with little effort. The republic of the seven Ionian Islands was placed under British protection; she gained possession of Malta and the Cape of Good Hope, and the colonies of Essequibo, Demerara, and Berbice. She also held Gibraltar, and thus confirmed that naval superiority which neither of the other powers called in question, especially as it had saved them from ruin and maintained their commercial resources.

One demand, indeed, was made by Britain which may be regarded as indicative of the dawn of a new era. The assent of the assembled powers to the abolition of the African slave-trade was asked and conceded. It was agreed that they should concert without loss of time such measures as were necessary to prevent the continuance of that inhuman traffic. In accordance with this determination was the naval victory which we gained at a time when the country was greatly impoverished, trade was almost at a stand-still, and the reaction following the close of years of war threatened not only general necessity, bankruptcy, and poverty, but, as a consequence, political and social disorder approaching to insurrection. There was something in the motive for which the Mediterranean fleet was again brought into action which served to elevate the spirit of the nation, and the rapidly gained and complete victory had much to do in raising the people from their despondency. The piracies, man-stealing, cruelties, and plunder which the Barbary States on the Mediterranean had been allowed to practise had been for ages a reproach to Christendom, and tales of the atrocities of the Barbary corsairs had been handed down from generation to generation, who had learned to regard "barbarian" as the equivalent of savage. The dread of the naval power of England had for a long time secured British ships and British subjects from the attacks of these pirates, and if, now and then, a British sailor was captured and sold into slavery, it was while serving under some foreign flag. Yet Britain determined to take measures at once to abate a monstrous evil from which she herself did not suffer and which she had no need to fear.

Early in the spring of 1816 Admiral Lord Exmouth, commanding in the Mediterranean, received orders to demand from the Beys of Tripoli and Tunis, and the Dey of Algiers, satisfaction and protection for the flags of the Ionian Isles, "which the Congress of Vienna had left under our protection," and the flags of Naples and Sardinia, together with the total abandonment of Christian slavery. Tripoli and Tunis were too weak to think of resisting, and implicitly complied. But the Dey of Algiers, relying on the great strength of his fortifications, offered only a partial satisfaction for past offences, and refused, or endeavoured to evade all promises for the future.

Before taking any steps in fulfilment of his instructions, Lord Exmouth made the arrangements necessary for an attack, which was to be the alternative if negotiations failed—a result to be expected at Algiers, which had hitherto withstood so many formidable armaments. His lordship ordered Captain Warde of the *Banterer* to proceed to Algiers, carefully to observe the town and the nature of its defences, to draw a plan of the works on the seaward side, to take soundings, and to make his observations on the anchorage. Lord Exmouth's instructions, written with his own hand, were an admirable illustration of the forethought with which he provided for every contingency, and which was the chief secret of his constant success. Captain Warde performed his difficult and important service with wonderful skill and secrecy.

The admiralty were greatly surprised when Lord Exmouth proposed to attack Algiers with only five sail of the line. Many naval officers, upon being consulted by the board, considered those works as altogether unassailable by ships. His lordship was offered any force he required, but he firmly adhered to his first demand; for he had satisfied himself that five ships could destroy the great fortifications on the mole as effectually as a greater number, and with far more safety to themselves. After he had explained his plans, and marked the position which every ship was to occupy, the admiralty allowed him to act upon his own judgment. "All will go well," said this brave sailor and most excellent man; "all will go well, as far at least as it depends on me. I know that nothing can resist a line-of-battle ship's fire."

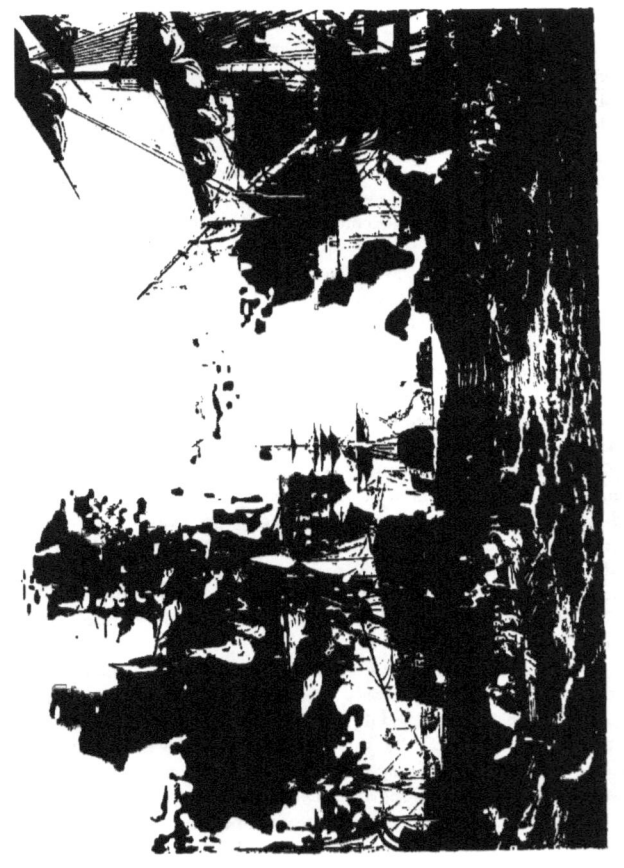

On the 9th of August the veteran was at Gibraltar. Here he found a Dutch squadron of five frigates and a corvette, commanded by Vice-admiral the Baron de Capellan, who, on learning the object of the expedition, solicited and obtained leave to co-operate. On Tuesday, the 27th of August, they came in sight of Algiers. As the ships lay becalmed Lord Exmouth sent Lieutenant Burgess in a boat, under a flag of truce, with the terms dictated by the prince regent, and a demand for the immediate liberation of the British consul and some other persons whom the dey had cast into prison. At eleven o'clock A.M. Lieutenant Burgess was met outside the mole by the captain of the port, who received the communication, and promised an answer in two hours. In the meantime a breeze springing up the fleet stood into the bay, and lay to, about a mile from the town. At two o'clock Lieutenant Burgess and the boat were seen returning with the signal that no answer had been given.

The admiral's ship, the *Queen Charlotte*, instantly telegraphed to the fleet, "Are you ready?" and the affirmative signal was immediately displayed from every ship. They all, English and Dutch frigates and ships of the line, bore up to their appointed stations. The *Queen Charlotte* led the attack. There was to be no firing from her until she came to anchor. The Algerines, confident in the strength of their works, also reserved their fire; indeed, they expected to carry the flag-ship by boarding her from their numerous gun-boats. The *Queen Charlotte* proceeded silently to her position; and at half-past two she anchored by the stern, just half a cable's length from the terrible mole-head.

The mole was crowded with troops, many of whom got upon the parapet to look at the ships; and Lord Exmouth, observing them as he stood upon the poop, waved to them to move away. As soon as the ship was fairly placed, and her cables stoppered, the crew gave three hearty cheers, such as Englishmen only can give. Scarcely had the sound of the last died away when a gun was fired from the upper tier of the eastern battery, and a second and a third followed in quick succession. One of the shots struck the *Superb*. At the first flash Lord Exmouth gave the order, "Stand by!" at the second, "Fire!" The report of the third gun was drowned in the thunder of the *Queen Charlotte's* broadside.

The Algerines replied with the fire of nearly 500 guns. The mole was filled with cannon, like the side of a line-of-battle ship, mostly disposed in a double tier, with ports below and embrasures above; but the eastern batteries next the lighthouse had an inner fortification with a third tier of guns, making sixty-six in these eastern batteries alone. These different batteries on the mole mounted altogether about 220 guns, eighteen being twenty-four or thirty-two pounders, and two of them being sixty-eight pounders, upwards of 20 feet long. All these guns were brought to bear point-blank upon Lord Exmouth's ships of the line. Some of his lordship's frigates and some of the Dutch frigates took up positions which three-deckers might have been justly proud of. There were a few bomb-vessels, whose shells were thrown with admirable precision by our marine artillery. There was no lack of courage and resolution on the part of the corsairs. Shortly after the commencement of the battle their flotilla of gunboats advanced to board the *Queen Charlotte* and the *Leander*. At first the smoke covered and concealed them, but so soon as they were seen a few well-directed shot sent thirty-three out of thirty-seven of these Algerine gun-boats to the bottom. At four o'clock a large Algerine frigate was boarded and set on fire. As she burst into a flame Lord Exmouth telegraphed to the fleet the animating signal, "Infallible!" Before seven o'clock all the vessels in port, except a brig and a schooner, were burning fast to the water's edge. As for the tremendous works on the mole-head, they had been ruined by the single fire of the *Queen Charlotte* a very few minutes after the combat had commenced. The fleet slackened their fire towards night, while the guns of the enemy became silent. Then the necessity was felt for husbanding the ammunition. The expenditure had been beyond all precedent. Our ships had fired nearly 118 tons of powder, and 50,000 shot, weighing more than 500 tons of iron, besides 960 thirteen and ten inch shells. Such a fire, close, concentrated, and well directed, nothing could resist. The mighty sea-defences of Algiers, with great part of the town itself, were shattered and crumbled to ruins.

As the night darkened the breeze freshened, and a tremendous storm of thunder and lightning came on, with torrents of rain; while the flaming ships and store-houses illuminated all the ruins on shore. In scarcely any former general action had the casualties been so great in proportion to the force employed. In the British ships 128 were killed and 690 wounded; and the Dutch, who had behaved most gallantly, had 13 killed and 52 wounded. The veteran commander-in-chief had a narrow escape; he was struck in three places, and a cannon-shot tore away the skirts of his coat, breaking one of the glasses and bending the rim of the spectacles in his pocket.

On the 28th, at daylight, Lieutenant Burgess was sent on shore with a flag of truce, and with the same demands he had carried the preceding morning; our bomb-vessels at the same time resuming their positions. Lord Exmouth was immediately given to understand that all his demands would be submitted to. On the morning of the 29th Captain Brisbane of the flag-ship went on shore, and had a conference with the humbled and astounded dey.

The negotiations were intrusted to Sir Charles Penrose. They were very short, for the Algerines could do nothing but submit and agree. The chief conditions were—the abolition of Christian slavery for ever; the surrender of all their slaves of whatever nation; and the dey's humble and public apology in person for the insult he had given to the British flag.

Three thousand Christians were delivered from slavery, and sent to their own countries and homes. Leaving a ship to receive a few more, Lord Exmouth sailed for England on the 3d of September. Scarcely Nelson himself had been in hotter fires than Exmouth, yet his lordship declared that he had never been under a fire so hot and terrible as this at Algiers. "The fire all round the mole," said he, "looked like Pandemonium. I never saw anything so grand and so *terrific;* for I was not on velvet for fear they would drive on board us. Their copper-bottoms floated full of fiery hot charcoal, and were red-hot above the surface, so that we could not hook on our fire-grapnels to put the boats to, and could do nothing but push out fire-booms, and spring the ship off by our warps, as occasion required. . . . I never saw any set of men more obstinate at their guns, and it was superior fire only that could keep them back. To be sure, nothing could stand before the *Queen Charlotte's* broadside. Everything fell before it; and the Swedish consul assures me we killed above 500 at the very first fire, from the crowded way in which their troops were drawn up, four deep above the gun-boats, which were also full of men. . . . I believe they are within bounds when they state their loss at 7000 men."

WILLIAM THE FOURTH.

At the beginning of the present century England had made great and rapid strides, not only in the development of her vast commercial resources, but in the direction of social and political reforms which advanced both civil and religious liberty. It was also a period during which such enormous progress was made in scientific discovery, in mechanical inventions, in the industrial arts, and in the apparatus of manufacture, that the resources of the country were indefinitely multiplied, and we seemed to enter upon a new era in which the fine arts, poetry, and general literature also advanced and were sustained by the growth of political freedom and by economic changes which encouraged the publication of numerous magazines and newspapers.

Of course the invention of steam machinery, and its increasing application to all kinds of industrial purposes, as well as to locomotion, were potent elements in these improvements. Not only was production enormously increased, but the means of rapid communication at once gave markets to the manufacturer, and brought food to the producer. In 1780 there were probably only about 13,800,000 inhabitants in Great Britain and Ireland, and the productive force was represented by the manual labour of about 32,000,000 labourers. In 1826 the population amounted to 22,500,000, while the productive power was equivalent to the labour of above 60,000,000 men. In 1769 our cotton manufactures did not exceed in annual value £200,000; in 1824 the annual value had risen to £33,500,000; in 1827 to £36,000,000; and in 1830 to little less than £40,000,000. In 1780 the quantity of coal raised for general use was about 2500 tons; in 1833 it was about 18,000,000 tons.

This was during the infancy of steam locomotion, and a still further enormous increase of trade and commerce followed the establishment of railways. Hitherto steam-boats on canals and rivers had formed the improved means for transit of goods and passengers. In 1830 the first great railway with locomotive engines, that between Liverpool and Manchester, was finished, and the success of the great experiment led to the immediate construction of other lines. The revolution caused by this wonderful invention was more complete than any that could have been effected by political combination or by the coalitions of European states. Even during an eventful year, the climax of a period of political excitement, when events were moving with rapidity towards complete constitutional freedom and the direct representation of the people in the legislature, the establishment of the railway system was recognized as a tremendous power on the side of the general advancement.

On the proclamation of William Henry, duke of Clarence, as King of England, no immediate alteration took place in the government, his majesty signifying to the Duke of Wellington and the ministers of his cabinet that he was anxious to retain their services. On Friday the 23d of July his majesty went in state to the House of Lords and prorogued parliament, the necessary dissolution was made next day by proclamation, and writs were ordered for the election of a new parliament, to be returnable on the 14th of September. A portion of the Whigs had been for some time contemplating a coalition with the Wellington and Peel party, but their advances were not met half-way, and the Whig party more resolutely than before took up the cry for reform.

On the 28th of July the revolution in Paris which ended in the abdication of Charles X. was hailed by the ultra-reformers in England as an event promising a new era in the history of nations. Public meetings were held to pass resolutions, commending the spirit with which the Parisians had shaken off encroaching despotism, deputations were sent to congratulate them on their triumph, and subscriptions were proposed to relieve the families of those citizens who had suffered in the cause. At some of these meetings, and in some of the more radical newspapers and other periodical publications, the people were called upon to consider how little was to be feared from military power, and how much could be done by pikes, barricades, and reversed coaches, carts, and omnibuses. As in the year 1790, the French declared that their revolution would make the tour of the globe. It very soon travelled into Belgium and into Poland, and its effects were felt in Italy, Saxony, Brunswick, Switzerland, and other countries. The Belgians had long been dissatisfied with their union with the Dutch, but that union might have lasted many a long year but for the events of Paris. On the 25th of August a riot broke out at Brussels which very soon assumed a character of political insurrection. The flame spread to

Liege, Namur, and other cities. The Dutch troops, numerically weak, could not maintain themselves in Brussels; that capital was evacuated after very little fighting, and Belgium was declared to be a separate and independent nation.

On the 8th of September the coronation of William IV. was solemnized in Westminster Abbey; and even on this occasion the change of times and fashions was marked by the plainness of the cortege and the simple but grand and solemn religious service of which the ceremony mainly consisted. The carriages which conveyed the king and his queen, Adelaide, from St. James' Palace to the abbey were the principal objects of attraction to the people assembled in the streets William wore his naval uniform, and this contributed to the satisfaction of his subjects as an appropriate token of our naval supremacy, and stimulated the hearty acclamations with which he was received.

Before the close of 1830 the demand for parliamentary reform had assumed a new character and aspect. It was no longer the mere war-cry of a political party, that could be silenced by contradictions or trivial concessions. It was no longer limited to the disfranchisement of a few close or corrupt boroughs, and the transference of the forfeited suffrage to certain towns and communities that were still unrepresented. Neither could it be postponed, as had hitherto been the case, to a more convenient season, when circumstances would be more favourable for change and the public mind in a more tranquil state for its accomplishment. These were the hopes of reasonable and yet ardent reformers; but there was a considerable difference between the views which were held by Earl Grey and the ministry and those of the people and their political leaders. When Lord John Russell attempted afterwards to introduce a wider measure the debates were prolonged and fierce, the second reading was only carried by a majority of one, and a division on a motion in the next debate left the ministry in a minority of eight.

On the assembling of the next parliament the king's speech, calling the attention of the legislature to the necessity for reform and for the adoption of measures to secure the prerogative of the crown, the authority of both houses of parliament, and the rights and liberties of the people, was applauded to the echo; and this elderly gentleman, who, with a certain good humour and plainness of address, had always been popular, was now cheered as the "Patriot King," the "Sailor King," and the friend of the people. These sentiments were somewhat

changed afterwards, when the opposition, led by Wellington, Mansfield, and Ellenborough, refusing to vote such changes in the constitution as the Reform Bill implied, the ministry resigned their office, and the king, unable to induce any statesman of influence to accept the post of prime minister, was compelled to ask Earl Grey and his adherents to return to power.

The whole country was then in a state of insurrection, and it was thought that the "bloodless revolution," by which Charles X. had just been compelled to relinquish the throne of France, might be repeated in England. But the Reform Bill was at length passed in the House of Lords, after fierce debate, during which not only London, but every important town in England, was in a state of wild excitement.

William was nearly sixty-five years old at the time of his accession, and may be said to have earned the title of "our Sailor King," inasmuch as all his public life had been in one way or another associated with the naval service. Before he was fourteen he had been rated a midshipman on board the *Prince George*, which soon after joined the Channel Fleet, under the command of Sir Charles Hardy, and at the end of the year (1779) sailed as one of the squadron sent out with Rodney to Gibraltar with supplies for the garrison. On the passage they fell in with a Spanish fleet of storeships under the convoy of seven men-of-war and took them all, twenty-two in number. The largest of these, the *Guipuscuano*, of eighty-four guns, Rodney named the *Prince William*, "in respect to his royal highness, in whose presence she had the honour to be taken." There was no fighting on that occasion, so that the prince could scarcely be said to have "smelt powder;" but eight days after, a Spanish squadron was encountered off Cadiz, and after a sharp engagement several of the enemy's ships were captured and the rest dispersed. Rodney then proceeded to the Bay of Gibraltar with his supplies, and stayed there for about three weeks, after which the *Prince George* returned in the division which, under Admiral Digby, took home the prizes, and his royal highness was once more in England, after completing his first expedition.

He subsequently made two or three short cruises and went again to Gibraltar with Admiral Darby, after which he sailed for New York with Admiral Digby, who commanded the *Prince George* and three other vessels. It was while he was lodging in the town during the winter that a plan was formed to seize him and carry him off, and though no such attempt was ever actually made, it was declared at the time that it was sanctioned by George Washington. In the autumn of 1782 he was, at his own request, transferred on board the *Warwick*, commanded by Captain Elphinstone, afterwards Lord Keith, but was soon afterwards removed by the king's orders to the *Barfleur*, under Sir Samuel, afterwards Lord Hood. It was while he was in this ship, when lying off Staten Island, that he first became acquainted with Nelson, for whom he always afterwards maintained a sincere friendship. After being stationed for some time at Jamaica and Havanah, his royal highness set out on a continental tour attended by General Bude and Captain Merrick. At Hanover he was joined by his brother Frederick, then styled Bishop of Osnaburg. The two princes visited Frederick the Great at Berlin, and spent a winter in Germany, after which William went alone to Switzerland, Savoy, Piedmont, and Prague, and thence to Italy, where he stayed the winter. On his return to England he passed his examination as lieutenant, and soon afterwards received a commission as captain of the *Pegasus*. In the following year, 1787, when he was twenty-two years of age, he was ordered to Jamaica, but took it upon himself to leave that station and return to Halifax, an act of insubordination for which he was ordered to Quebec, but he again committed a breach of discipline by leaving that place and sailing for England. On his arrival at Cork he was ordered to Plymouth, where he received instructions not to leave without permission, and it was determined to keep him there for as long a time as he had improperly absented himself from his station, after which he was to return to Halifax and the West Indies. This sentence was carried out by his being appointed to the command of the *Andromeda*, in which he remained, principally at Jamaica, till the spring of 1789. It was impossible to permit a prince to set so bad an example, and it was difficult to determine how he should be punished for any probable insubordination in future, so on his return he was raised to the peerage as Duke of Clarence and St. Andrews, and Earl of Munster, with an income of £12,000 a year settled upon him by act of parliament. The next year, however, he commanded the *Valiant* for some time, and on that ship being paid off was made rear-admiral of the blue. In 1793 he was promoted to be rear-admiral of the red; in 1794, vice-admiral of the blue; in 1795, vice-admiral of the red. In 1799 he was admiral of the blue, and in 1801 became admiral of the fleet. During all this time, however, he stayed at home, and from 1797 usually residing at Bushey Park, of which he was made ranger. Two years after he had returned home from his voyage in the *Andromeda*, that is to say in 1791, he had formed a connection with the celebrated Mrs. Jordan, which continued for twenty years, during which time five sons and five daughters were born to them. The eldest son was created Duke of Munster, the eldest daughter was Lady Delisle.

Mrs. Jordan, whose real name was Dorothy Bland (Jordan being only an assumed or stage name), was an accomplished, facile, and charming actress, whose great attraction was a certain sprightly simplicity. Hazlitt says: "Her face, her tones, her manner were irresistible. Her smile had the effect of sunshine, and her laugh did one good to hear it. Her voice was eloquence itself; it seemed as if her heart were always at her mouth. She was all gaiety, openness, and good nature. She rioted in her fine animal spirits, and gave more pleasure than any other actress because she had the greatest spirit of enjoyment in herself. In 1785 she first appeared before a London audience at Drury Lane as "Peggy" in "The Country Girl," and immediately became famous, receiving an enthusiastic welcome wherever she appeared. When the Duke of Clarence first made overtures to her she was the mistress of a Mr. Ford, who refused to marry her because he feared the displeasure of his father. She then accepted the proposals of the duke, and for the long period already mentioned appears to have lived with him in domestic harmony. A yearly allowance of £4400 was settled on her for the maintenance of herself and her daughters, with a provision that if she should ever return to the stage the care of the four daughters and the £1500 a year allowed for them should revert to his royal highness. Suddenly, in 1811, and not long after this arrangement was made, she expressed a wish to resume her profession. It would perhaps be idle and unprofitable to attempt to explain the motives for the remarkable and sudden change that took place; but it is certain that the four children and the allowance for their maintenance were surrendered to their royal father, that she retired to France in great sorrow and embarrassment, and five years afterwards, on the 3d of July, 1816, died in a state of extreme mental affliction at St. Cloud.

On the 11th of July, 1818, the duke was married at Kew to the Princess Adelaide Louisa Theresa Caroline Amelia, eldest daughter of George Frederic Charles, duke of Saxe-Meiningen. Upon his marriage £6000 per annum was added to his income, and in 1827, when by the death of the Duke of York he became heir-presumptive to the throne, a further increase of £3000 was made to his annual allowance, and £6000 a year was settled upon the duchess.

Prince William was then sixty-two years of age, and on the elevation of Mr. Canning to the premiership he was placed at the head of the admiralty, but without a seat in the cabinet. He held the position no longer than for six months, and then returned to private life, until, on the death of George IV., he succeeded to the throne. It was never thought that William, duke of Clarence, displayed any remarkable capacity, though he frequently took part in the debates in the House of Lords, where he was a moderately fluent, though a not very elegant or logical speaker. He chiefly displayed his oratorical ability in his determined opposition to the abolition of slavery, and for some years this detracted very seriously from his popularity, until what may almost be called the accident of his political association with those ministers who promoted the Reform Bill placed him nominally at the head of the Liberal interest. That William IV. was personally favourable to a large measure of reform, however, there can be little doubt, and he at least possessed one important qualification in a sovereign who found himself at once popular and liable to those suspicions and changes of public opinion which in troublous and incendiary times are frequently terrifying symptoms of revolution. He seems to have been a stout-hearted old gentleman, who was able to keep his temper and preserve a certain sturdiness of demeanour even in the midst of what threatened to be a political conflagration. Even when Earl Grey went to him to ask him to create such a number of Liberal peers as would form a majority in the upper house, and so carry the Reform Bill, he showed no immediate weakness of purpose, but after a night's consideration declared he could not consent to this course. He thought the anti-reform peers very obstinate and very wrong, but he did not like making a dangerous precedent. The Lords would say he had swamped their house. The alternative of the resignation of the ministry was accepted, and though he afterwards found it impossible to form another cabinet, and the excitement of the country made it necessary for him to assemble parliament again by recalling the former ministry, he submitted to the humiliation with something like dignity, and without the exhibition of dismay which the threatened loss of his own popularity might have excused.

Lord Lyndhurst had been unable to find a statesman who would act as premier. The Duke of Wellington, who had had his windows smashed by the rioters and was the subject of much popular execration, which he long outlived, to become once more the popular hero of England's great military triumphs, was willing to do anything for the king, but was by no means desirous of taking office. Sir Robert Peel refused to become prime minister, as he felt he could be of no service to the king or to the country at that juncture, and as he was still opposed to any extensive alteration of the constitution. All that the opposition peers could do they afterwards did. When the Grey ministry was restored and the Reform Bill was passed in the upper house they were out of their places:—their seats were mostly empty, as were also the cross or independent benches. The first meeting of the reformed parliament was of itself an important era in our history. This great national representation had undergone not a partial but a complete change. The first important struggle, in the seventeenth century, had been to reduce the royal authority below the level of parliament; the second, which had just succeeded, was to elevate the authority of the Commons above that of the Lords, and to constitute the house of the former the real governing power of the empire. The alterations which had been made in popular representation were such as the reform appeared to necessitate. Of these the greatest was in the county constituencies of England. Formerly there had been fifty-two, which returned ninety-four members; but now, by the division of counties, these constituencies were increased to eighty-two, which returned 159 members. As all boroughs having less than a population of 2000 were to be disfranchised, fifty-six of these, which had returned 111 members, were no longer represented. Such boroughs as had a population of less than 4000, and had sent two representatives, were now only to return one, and under this category thirty seats were made vacant. As the number of members that composed the House of Commons was not to be diminished, these 143 constituencies were transferred to the towns and districts that had increased in population and importance. In like manner, while no change was made upon Ireland, Scotland retained her former number of representatives, but with changes adapted to the increase of the population in new localities, and its diminution in the old. The mode of election was also simplified in town and country both as to the time occupied and the registration of voters, as also the qualifications for a vote, inhabitants of towns being entitled to the franchise who paid £10 of yearly rental, and of the counties copyholders and leaseholders to the value of 40s. In this way it was attempted to combine the privileges of the old agricultural and the new mercantile England; to reconcile the moneyed with the hereditary aristocracy; and so to extend the right of election as to make the House of Commons what it claimed to be, the representation of the bulk of the people as well as of worth and intelligence.

The first harsh notes which sounded in the new parliament were caused by the reception given by Mr. Daniel O'Connell to that part of the address on the king's speech which related to the terrible disturbances in Ireland, and throughout the course of the subsequent debate Irish members continued to complain of measures which, though they were afterwards passed, were considerably mitigated in their stringency by other measures of redress and improvement. Perhaps the most prominently historical measure first passed by the reformed parliament was the Emancipation Act, by which negro slavery was gradually abolished in our West Indian possessions. If anything could cloud the joy of such an event it was the circumstance that only thirty-one days before the Emancipation Act passed, Wilberforce, its author and champion, had died. But he was cheered with the assurance that the beloved project of his life was safe, and that in a few days the bill would become law.

The session was also distinguished for the enormous advances made in the direction of commercial freedom. A renewal of the bank charter was the occasion for important amendments in the organization of the Bank of England; a renewal of the East India Company's charter threw open to all British subjects a trade which had till then been a gigantic monopoly; and a free-trade commission was sent over to France. Efforts were made to inquire into and improve the condition of our labouring classes, the Factory Bill was fully and carefully discussed, and an act was passed regulating the hours of labour for children in factories, and providing for their education. Taxation was reduced a million and a half, and the Municipal Regulation Act, a sweeping measure of corporation reform, completed in the boroughs the improvements which had been contemplated by the provisions of the clauses of the Reform Bill.

HER MOST GRACIOUS MAJESTY QUEEN VICTORIA.

It is not easy to write on the subject of the life and character of our Queen—first, because during her long reign she has so held the hearts of her people to loyal and loving appreciation of her virtues, that words which would at all adequately express even the common opinion, would read like an attempt to eulogize a woman who is too truly womanly to endure flattery, and too penetrating a judge of praise to seek it in the adulations of picked sentences and courtly phrases. Secondly, because the sweet and simple chronicles of some part of her early life, written by the Queen herself in *The Early Days of the Prince Consort* and *Our Life in the Highlands*, have conveyed to thousands of readers a better picture of the royal household, better portraits of its members, and more interesting records of the daily life which alternated between serious duties of state and simple gladsome recreations, than can be repeated by any other hand. When to these volumes are added *The Life of the Prince Consort*, now only just completed under the supervision of Her Majesty, and with many explanatory notes contributed by herself, the biography, which is also an autobiography, is so complete as to need little addition, while its evident sincerity carries to every heart a confirmation of the respect and affection with which Victoria is regarded by her subjects.

The accession of the youthful daughter of the Duke of Kent to the throne, after the death of William IV. on the 20th of June, 1837, was regarded with a kind of delighted curiosity by all classes of the people. The fact of a pure and simple-minded girl of eighteen, who had hitherto lived in domestic seclusion, being called to a position of such great responsibility at once awakened a tender loyalty which gave to the country a tone of devoted feeling and noble ardour.

It was known that the young princess, the fatherless daughter of the Duke of Kent, had been well fitted by early training, by education, and by natural disposition to be queen of a country where freedom "broadens down from precedent to precedent." The people, tired of continued strife, longed for peace. The records of the courts of the Georges had so often been of a nature to revolt and to disgust the nation that there was a general sense of relief and of happy expectation that the youthful sovereign would be the representative of a purer and better order, free from the evil influences that had debased royalty, and made history itself a mere small-beer chronicle of vile intrigues and petty wranglings among partizans and favourites. A tender regard slid into the hearts of men and women by whom loyalty was interpreted to mean a personal attachment to the sovereign. Not only respect for the crown, but affection for the queen stirred into emotion what had hitherto been only political fidelity; and even those who, in the extreme views which they professed, seemed to care little for royalty or for "the throne" as an institution, spoke with gentle regard of the young, intelligent, and innocent sovereign who was to exercise so beneficial an influence on society.

After the death of the Duke of Kent in 1820 the duchess had entirely devoted herself to the nurture and instruction of her daughter, the future queen, and she was well qualified for the duty. Her first husband was Duke of Leinengen, and she was sister to Leopold, King of the Belgians, one of the most sagacious and accomplished of European princes. The Princess Victoria became an excellent musician, acquired a considerable knowledge of modern languages, and even some proficiency in Latin, her dislike of which she has recorded with amusing *naiveté*. She was also well instructed in scientific subjects, especially in botany, and possessed no little talent as an artist. Her general education was superior to that of most young ladies of her age, even in the highest ranks of society; and her brightness and intelligence enabled her to continue her studies long after she had ascended the throne, and to pursue some of them with the delightful aid of the accomplished and cultured prince whose studies and acquirements so admirably fitted him to be her royal husband. The simple mode of living adopted by the Duchess of Kent was accompanied by regular and frequent exercise, and the princess was a famous equestrian, and took great pleasure in yachting excursions, her mother having overcome her own timidity in order to cultivate the greater courage and address of her daughter in those amusements which belong to the robust English life. Thus the excellent constitution of the princess enabled her to become a representative of that healthy womanhood which is regarded as a national characteristic.

It should not be forgotten that the youthful queen had also studied the principles of the English laws and constitution under the tuition of Lord Viscount Melbourne, who, if not practically a very great statesman, was one of the ablest exponents of the subjects in which it was necessary that the future sovereign should be instructed.

The affectionate regard as well as the sincere and joyful anticipations of the people of England seemed to find satisfaction in the expressions which were used by the queen, when, in clear and unfaltering tones, she made her first declaration. To what extent the actual words of that declaration may be attributed to her own choice it was never necessary to inquire. It was evident by the emphasis she gave them that she understood, and intended seriously to adopt their meaning when she said:—

"This awful responsibility is imposed upon me so suddenly, and at so early a period of my life, that I should feel myself utterly oppressed by the burden were I not sustained by the hope that divine Providence, which has called me to this work, will give me strength for the performance of it, and that I shall find in the purity of my intentions, and in my zeal for the public welfare, that support and those resources which usually belong to a more mature age and to long experience. I place my firm reliance upon the wisdom of parliament, and upon the loyalty and affection of my people. I esteem it also a peculiar advantage that I succeed to a sovereign whose constant regards for the rights and liberties of his subjects, and whose desire to promote the amelioration of the laws and institutions of the country, have rendered his name the object of general attachment and veneration. Educated in England under the tender and enlightened care of a most affectionate mother, I have learned from my infancy to respect and love the constitution of my native country. It will be my unceasing study to maintain the reformed religion as by law established, securing at the same time to all, the full enjoyment of religious liberty: and I shall promote to the utmost of my power the happiness and welfare of all classes of my subjects."

This was the speech delivered to the first council, which was called immediately after the death of William IV. at twenty minutes after two o'clock on the morning of the 21st June, 1837. At eleven o'clock the youthful queen had to meet the council at Kensington Palace, and the simple and gracious dignity which was conspicuous in so young a sovereign won all hearts. Even a writer whose records in his recently published journals are nearly always satirical or cynical, and are sometimes almost brutal in their expressions, was either carried away in spite of his habitual caution, or felt that he could not there entertain the suspicious and depreciatory temper which perhaps his experience as clerk of the council had provoked. His language, in speaking of the young queen, in the diary only recently published, is so earnest as almost to rise to enthusiasm, though, even in a journal which was not to be made public till after his death, he is careful to guard against being accused of partiality. He says:—

"Never was anything like the first impression she produced, or the chorus of praise and admiration which is raised about her manner and behaviour, and certainly not without justice. It was very extraordinary, and something far beyond what was looked for. Her extreme youth and inexperience, and the ignorance of the world concerning her, naturally excited intense curiosity to see how she would act on this trying occasion; and there was a considerable assemblage at the palace, notwithstanding the short notice which was given. The first thing to be done was to teach her her lesson, which, for this purpose, Melbourne had himself to learn. I gave him the council papers, and explained all that was to be done, and he went and explained all this to her. He asked her if she would enter the room accompanied by the great officers of state, but she said she would come in alone. When the lords were assembled the lord-president informed them of the king's death, and suggested as they were so numerous that a few of them should repair to the presence of the queen, and inform her of the event, and that their lordships were assembled in consequence, and accordingly the two royal dukes (Cumberland and Sussex, the Duke of Cambridge being at Hanover), the two archbishops, the chancellor, and Melbourne went with him. The queen received them in the adjoining room alone. As soon as they had returned the proclamation was read and the usual order passed, when the doors were thrown open and the queen entered, accompanied by her two uncles, who advanced to meet her. She bowed to the lords, took her seat, and then read the speech in a clear, distinct, and audible voice, and without any appearance of fear or embarrassment. She was quite plainly dressed, and in mourning. After she had read her speech, and taken and signed the oath for the security of the Church of Scotland, the privy-councillors were sworn, the two dukes first by themselves; and as these two old men, her uncles, knelt before her, swearing allegiance and kissing her hand, I saw her blush up to the eyes, as if she felt the contrast between their civil and natural relations, and this was the only sign of emotion which she evinced. Her manner to them was very graceful and engaging: she kissed them both, and rose from her chair, and moved towards the Duke of Sussex, who was farthest from her, and too infirm to reach her. She seemed rather bewildered at the multitude of men who were sworn, and who came one after another to kiss her hand; but she did not speak to anybody, nor did she make the slightest difference in her manner, or show any in her countenance to any individual of any rank, station, or party. I particularly watched her when Melbourne, and the ministers, and the Duke of Wellington, and Peel approached her. She went through the whole ceremony, occasionally looking at Melbourne for instruction when she had any doubt what to do, which hardly ever occurred, and with perfect calmness and self-possession, but at the same time with a graceful modesty and propriety particularly interesting and ingratiating. Peel afterwards said how amazed he was at her manner and behaviour, at her apparent deep sense of her situation, her modesty, and, at the same time, her firmness."[1]

It is forty years since the young girl of eighteen made her declaration to the council, and the queen, who can now stand amidst her children and grandchildren, has retained the loyal affections of a people to whom she might appeal with a confidence as unfaltering as that of her girlhood repeating the words of promise, the obligations of which she has so well fulfilled. Can any queen take higher rank or truer sovereignty than this?

It is more than twenty-five years since the poet-laureate in a "Dedication," wrote:—

——" May you rule us long,
" And leave us rulers of your blood
As noble till the latest day !
May children of our children say,
'She wrought her people lasting good.

"' Her court was pure; her life serene;
God gave her peace, her land reposed;
A thousand claims to reverence closed
In her as Mother, Wife, and Queen.

[1] Greville, *Journals of the Reigns of George IV. and William IV.*

> "'And statesmen at her council met,
> Who knew the seasons when to take
> Occasion by the hand, and make
> The bounds of freedom wider yet.
>
> "'By shaping some august decree,
> Which kept her throne unshaken still,
> Broad-based upon her people's will,
> And compass'd by the inviolate sea.'"

Alas! the serenity and repose of the domestic life of our queen was shaken by the great sorrow which befell her ten years after these verses were written. The claims to reverence which closed in her as mother, wife, and queen remain; though both she and the people have had to mourn the loss of the prince who was her consort, and shared with her the affection and regard of the nation.

The young queen had reigned only two years and a half when she announced to the council assembled at Buckingham Palace her intention of contracting a matrimonial alliance with Prince Francis Charles Augustus Albert Emmanuel, of Saxe-Coburg-Gotha, second son of Duke Ernest, the first and younger brother of the Duke of Saxe-Coburg-Gotha. The formal announcement of these stately titles were but accessories to the high rank of those who were about to be allied in a marriage which was one of mutual affection and unbiassed choice. The prince, who was of the same age as the queen, had become naturalized a few days before the royal marriage, which took place on the 10th of February, 1840; and he soon became so completely identified with England and the English, that he could scarcely have been more truly allied to the people if he had been educated at Oxford or Cambridge instead of at the University of Bonn, where he was an accomplished student.

Perhaps there never was a prince, even of an English royal family, who became more familiar and more thoroughly acceptable to the people than the Consort, who is now so often spoken of as "Albert the Good;" but then few, if any princes of our royal houses, have been at once so thoroughly imbued with the spirit of English simple domestic life, or have taken so practical and genuine an interest in social improvements, and the development of those industrial and economical arts which are associated with the commercial prosperity of the country. Another important element in the popularity of Prince Albert, was the remarkable tact and discretion with which he sustained his position as the

beloved and trusted husband of the queen, without becoming enmeshed in political or state affairs. It is quite possible that his keen faculty of observation, and his quiet reflective wisdom, were not without their influence on the opinions both of the queen and of some of the statesmen who enjoyed his friendship; but his opinions were never obtruded, and probably were never offered except when they were asked for. At the same time, the whole course of his public life furnishes evidence that they would always have been in accordance with the progress of free institutions and the welfare of the people.

There is no need to dwell here upon the sorrow which fell upon the queen and the nation when one so beloved was removed in the midst of his beneficent and yet modest work, on the 14th of December, 1861. In the period of grief and suffering which followed, the sympathies of the people of England were with their sovereign, and it is not too much to say, that in the long retirement occasioned by the lasting sorrow of her bereavement, the memory of the great loss which she and they had sustained enabled her subjects to respect her continued seclusion, even though they heartily desired her return to public life. Now that her majesty has on several occasions appeared once more among her people in London and elsewhere, the multitudes who fill the streets and the earnest greetings with which she is welcomed attest that the affectionate loyalty of the country is unimpaired.

Upon the vast changes, the superb achievements, the enormous advances, which have characterized the reign of a sovereign who for more than forty years has retained the love of her people and the respect of every ruler and every court in Europe, we cannot find space to speak. The history of the reign of Victoria is the history of a great national epoch, in which the queen has held a foremost place. The years of her widowhood have been passed in frequent retirement from public life, but not in actual seclusion. Whether she be in the pleasant retreat of Osborne in the Isle of Wight, or in the remoter palace at Balmoral, endeared to her by those recollections which are shared alike by her English and the Scottish subjects, she is known to her people; and her voice is still potent for good, her judgment still listened to with respect, her influence still felt both in the councils of the state and in the social life which her example has helped to purify and to elevate.

HIS ROYAL HIGHNESS ALBERT, PRINCE CONSORT.

FRANCIS CHARLES AUGUSTUS ALBERT EMMANUEL—who as "Prince Albert," or the "Prince Consort"—was to become almost representatively English, and to share with the queen herself the respectful affection and esteem of the English people, was the second son of Ernest, Duke of Saxe-Coburg, Saalfield, and of his wife Louise, daughter of Augustus, Duke of Saxe-Gotha-Altenburg. He was born on the 26th of August, 1819, his elder and only brother Ernest, having been born on the 21st of June in the previous year. The two boys were named after the two sons of Frederick the Gentle, Elector of Saxony, who were carried off from the Castle of Altenburg in 1455 by Kunz of Kaufungen, but were afterwards recovered and became the founders of the two branches of the Saxon family. Both the young princes were distinguished for their precocity, and for their good qualities, and they remained almost inseparable until they had reached the respective ages of twenty and nineteen years of age. They had been at college together, studied under the same tutors, taken the same voyages, and shared the same domestic life; so that when it had become necessary for the elder, Ernest, to enter upon his military duties at Dresden, as a preparation for his succession to the dukedom, the parting of the brothers was a sorrowful one. "The separation," wrote Prince Albert to their old comrade and fellow-student, Prince von Löwenstein, on the 26th of October, 1838, "will be frightfully painful to us. Until now we have never, as long as we can recollect, been a single day away from each other."

The house of Coburg was intimately allied by marriage with the royal family of England. In 1816 Prince Leopold, the youngest brother of Prince Albert's father, the Duke of Coburg, had married the Princess Charlotte, who was already the darling of the English people because of her beauty and innocence, and because they hoped in her to see the restoration of purity and dignity to the English throne. Her husband, a wise, virtuous, and accomplished prince, was scarcely less admired and beloved, and the sudden calamity of her death on the

5th of November, 1817, in less than a year after their union, drove him to a voluntary though only a temporary exile. The untimely death of the Duke of Kent, within eight months after the birth of the Princess Victoria, threw upon his brother-in-law, Prince Leopold, the care of his widow and child. The little "Mayflower," as the German relatives had already named the princess, was therefore naturally regarded with peculiar interest by the family at Coburg, and long before she could have been regarded as the future Queen of England (that is, during the time that Queen Adelaide might still hope to have children to take the place of those whom she had lost), the idea of her marriage with one of her Coburg cousins had obviously been so distinctly entertained, that Prince Albert's nurse was in the habit of prattling to him, when he was only three years old, about his destined bride in England.[1]

From childhood Prince Albert was distinguished for personal beauty, and for that winning sincerity which, united with considerable attainments, great self-control, and a remarkably sound judgment, so eminently qualified him for the position that he afterwards acquired in this country. Of his character, disposition, and judgment, his uncle Leopold had a very high opinion, and Leopold himself was one of the most accomplished, as he was one of the most astute and judicious, advisers in Europe, even before he accepted the throne of Belgium. It was doubtless a great loss to the young prince that his mother had been separated from his father by divorce, while he and his brother were yet infants; but the dowager duchess was yet living, a woman in every respect distinguished, warm-hearted, possessing a powerful understanding, and loving her grandchildren most tenderly. However, the boys had been transferred, while they were yet mere infants (the elder being less than five years old), to the care of a tutor, M. Florschutz of Coburg, who continued for many years to superintend their studies with conscientious zeal. In 1824 the separation of the duke and duchess took place, followed in 1826 by a divorce, so that the grandmother and the step-grandmother (second wife of the maternal grandfather) were chiefly concerned in the domestic nurture of the children.

In 1836 it became almost certain that the Princess Victoria must soon succeed to the throne, and there were already several aspirants to her hand in the various courts of Europe. It was necessary, therefore, for King Leopold, who had by that time accepted the throne

[1] *Life of the Prince Consort;* by Theodore Martin.

of Belgium, and was regarded as the most sagacious of living sovereigns, to discover what were the inclinations of his niece, and to act with the greatest caution, lest he should unconsciously lead her to a decision to which he had no desire to influence her, although he would have regarded it with satisfaction. That he sincerely hoped for an alliance between his nephew of Saxe-Coburg and his niece of Britain there can be no doubt, but he was delicately careful not to precipitate an engagement. In order to be thoroughly impartial he sought the aid and counsel of an adviser as astute and as independent as himself, the famous Baron Christian Friedrich von Stockmar, who seems thenceforward to have devoted himself to the service of the princess who was soon to be Queen of England, and to have watched her deepest interests by carefully noting and afterwards confidentially advising and directing the studies and the occupations of the prince who was at no distant date to become her husband. Baron Stockmar, who was a native of Coburg, had entered the service of Prince Leopold as private physician at the time of the prince's marriage with the Princess Charlotte. She had died with her hand clasped in his, and it was he who had to announce to the prince the blow which struck him to the heart both in his affections and his ambition. By his sympathy and skilful treatment the prince had been enabled to sustain a shock under which he might otherwise have sunk. From this time to 1831 Stockmar had acted as the prince's private secretary and controller of his household, residing almost exclusively in England, where he acquired a thorough knowledge of the country, its people, and constitution, and bringing to the study of these the sympathy of strong liberal opinions, together with powers of observation and philosophical deduction of a very high order. He had taken part, as the private adviser and representative of King Leopold, in the protracted and complex diplomatic negotiations with the plenipotentiaries of the great European powers, which took place in London after the king's acceptance of the Belgian crown, and which resulted in the treaty of 1831. He had, therefore, been in intimate contact with the leading diplomats of Europe as well as with the chiefs of the two great political parties in England, and by all, his unusual abilities, his single-mindedness, and sturdy integrity were held in high estimation. "C'est un original," said Count Félix de Merode, "mais quel honnête homme!" And Lord Palmerston, no friendly critic, declared: "I have come, in my life, across only one absolutely disinterested man—Stockmar!"[1]

This was the counsellor to whom King Leopold applied, and he could not have had a better one in the interests of the princess herself, to whom he seems to have had a deep and loyal attachment, which made him jealously anxious in his close observation of the character, conduct, and disposition of the prince who was to become her husband. It is certain that the austere sincerity with which he answered the appeal for his advice was the happiest omen for the welfare of the objects of his solicitude. In a letter to the King of the Belgians in 1836, he wrote:—"Albert is a fine young fellow, well-grown for his age, with agreeable and valuable qualities, and who, if things go well, may, in a few years, turn out a handsome man of a kindly, simple, yet dignified demeanour. Externally, therefore, he possesses all that pleases the sex, and at all times and in all countries must please. It may prove, too, a lucky circumstance that even now he has something of an English look. But now the question is, How as to his mind? On this point, too, one hears much to his credit. But these judgments are all more or less partial; and until I have observed him longer I can form no judgment as to his capacity and the probable development of his character. He is said to be circumspect, discreet, and even now cautious. But all this is not enough. He ought to have not merely great ability, but a *right* ambition and great force of will as well. To pursue for a lifetime a political career so arduous demands more than energy and inclination, it demands also that earnest frame of mind which is ready of its own accord to sacrifice mere pleasure to real usefulness. If he is not satisfied hereafter with having achieved one of the most influential positions in Europe, how often will he feel tempted to repent what he has undertaken? If he does not from the very outset accept it as a vocation of grave responsibility, on the efficient fulfilment of which his honour and happiness depend, there is small likelihood of his succeeding." One thing above all he urged as indispensable, that no claim for the hand of his cousin should be preferred unless an impression in his favour from personal acquaintance should first have been produced.

In May, 1836, the Duke of Saxe-Coburg came to England with his two sons and remained for four weeks. Of course the probability

[1] *Life of the Prince Consort;* by Theodore Martin.

of an alliance had so often been mentioned to the prince in earlier days, that he could scarcely be unconscious of the possible object of the visit, but he had no reason to think that this was more than a desire on the part of his family, and the Princess Victoria was left free to follow her own inclination. That this inclination was in accordance with that of King Leopold soon became manifest; for when his majesty afterwards made the princess aware of his wishes, she at once responded by writing: "I have only now to beg you, my dearest uncle, to take care of the health of one now so dear to me, and to take him under your special protection." Nothing certain was made known to the prince, however, though his studies were directed in accordance with the probable position which he was afterwards to occupy. By the advice of Stockmar he and his brother went to Brussels, where their uncle was working out the problem of constitutional government. Berlin was regarded by this wise adviser as a bad political school, and the manners of the city were profligate; Vienna occupied a position in relation to Germany which made it an undesirable place for the education of a German prince; the training at universities was too scholastic, one-sided, and theoretical for one who had to study men and the course of political events in the free arena of a constitutional kingdom. At Brussels the young men were placed under the care of Baron Wiechmann, a retired officer of the English-German legion, for the study of history and modern languages, and also under the tuition of M. Quetelet, the eminent statist and mathematician. With this gentleman the prince continued to correspond until the last year of his life, and he frequently expressed his acknowledgments of the influence which the teaching he had received from him exercised in relation to many important subjects.

From Brussels the young men went to Bonn, and here Prince Albert pursued his studies with great eagerness, devoting himself particularly to the natural sciences and political economy. "Amongst all the young men at the university," writes Prince William of Löwenstein, with whom he there formed a close and intimate friendship, "he was distinguished by his knowledge, his diligence, and his amiable bearing in society." Along with his severer studies he kept up his physical training, and in a fencing match carried off the prize from about thirty competitors, and he also continued to make the study of music one of his most cherished recreations, having already shown considerable gifts as a composer. While he was at Bonn the death of William IV. gave to the Princess Victoria the grave responsibilities of royalty —responsibilities which the hostile struggles of political parties for place and power made still more serious.

The accession of the queen, of course, revived the rumours which had for some time been current of a contemplated marriage with her cousin, and in order to withdraw public attention from the princes King Leopold advised that they should spend the autumn of 1837 in that tour through Switzerland and Italy to which reference has already been made. On his return to Bonn Prince Albert resumed his studies, and at the end of the year it was thought desirable to bring the subject of the marriage explicitly before him. King Leopold thought that some decisive arrangement should be made for the year 1839; but to this the young queen demurred. Both she and the prince were too young, she said, and as they were both under age, her subjects would regard their marriage as premature, while the prince was yet but imperfectly acquainted with the English language, and required not only a wider experience, but more practised habits of observation, than he had then acquired. King Leopold offered no objection to these prudent representations, and stated the whole case honestly and kindly to the prince, who, on his part, regarded the subject from a high and honourable point of view, though he naturally required a promise that during the long delay proposed he should have some certain ground of assurance, since, in the event of the queen no longer desiring the marriage, he would be placed in a ridiculous position, and his prospects for the future would be seriously injured.

It was subsequently arranged that he should make a tour in Italy to complete his education, accompanied, at the request of the queen, by Baron Stockmar. In Florence he continued his studies, living a simple life even in the midst of the gay and brilliant society in which he was a welcome guest. Rising at six in the morning he worked till mid-day, when he partook of a plain dinner, seldom drinking anything but water, and going to bed as a rule at nine o'clock. His chief recreation was music, and the fine organ of the Church of the Badia afforded him frequent opportunities for practice at times when the building was closed to the public. Sir Francis Seymour writes: "The monks, on their way to the refectory, would stop and listen, whispering to each other 'Quel Principe forestiere suona bene quasi quanto il nostro Papi'—Papi being the organist of the Badia, and the prince's private instructor.

From Florence the prince went to Rome, and thence returned to Milan, taking Leghorn, Lucca, and Genoa on the way. At Milan he was met by his father, with whom he returned to Coburg by way of Geneva, to be present at the celebration of his brother's coming of age on the 21st June, 1839. By a special act of the legislature Prince Albert was declared to be of age at the same time. He had hoped to return home in order to resume those studies in political and social economy which Stockmar had advised him to pursue in conjunction with his acquisition of a further knowledge of the English language and history. Instead of this, however, he had to accompany his father to Carlsbad, and after a short interval of quiet and regular occupation at Rosenau, prepared for a visit to England. That visit was undertaken with the erroneous impression that the youthful queen "wished the affair to be considered as broken off, and that for four years she could think of no marriage"—such were the words of the prince in a letter to Prince Löwenstein, and such was the impression conveyed by the representations of King Leopold in accordance with the letter which he had received from her majesty desiring delay. Those representations were, perhaps, more unpromising than her majesty intended, for her early inclination had undergone no change, and, to use her own words, "she never had an idea, if she married at all, of any one else."

While the queen sought to defer their union, and the prince desired, while yielding to her representations, to receive some assurance from her that he was not waiting in vain, there were many external reasons for her early marriage. Not only were various diplomatic intriguers so anxious for the disposal of her hand in the interests of their own ambitious schemes, that their pretensions had become both personally annoying and publicly disquieting; but social and political questions were affected by that strife of parties which arose from squabbles about the personal influence of those by whom her majesty was surrounded, and to whom she not unnaturally felt the attachment that proceeds from personal regard and confidence. It was not easy for her to separate this regard for Lord Melbourne and for some of his adherents from an appearance of political partisanship which was beginning to be mischievous. It was difficult for a young and ingenuous woman, scarcely past girlhood, to adopt the astute advice even of such a wise counsellor as the King of the Belgians, and only a rare intelligence and an honesty of nature still more rare could have enabled so young a sovereign to maintain the integrity of her intentions, especially amidst a life of dazzling excitement which the queen herself has described to be "detrimental to all natural feelings and affections."[1] Those who had the welfare of the young queen most at heart were anxious to secure for her without delay a husband's guidance and support, and with it that domestic tranquillity which would be most effectual in promoting her happiness.

The attainment of both these objects was nearer than either of the persons principally concerned seem to have imagined. On the 10th of October, 1839, the prince arrived with his brother at Windsor Castle. The three years which had passed since their previous visit to England had greatly improved their personal appearance. General Grey says: "Tall and manly as they both were, Prince Albert was eminently handsome. But there was also in his countenance a gentleness of expression and peculiar sweetness in his smile, with a look of deep thought and high intelligence in his clear blue eye and expansive forehead that added a charm to the impression he produced in those who saw him far beyond that derived from mere beauty and regularity of features."

With the attractions of personal appearance Prince Albert possessed not only considerable mental endowments and varied accomplishments, but a remarkable humour, which was displayed both in his talent for drawing and in his conversation to intimate friends. Stockmar, writing of him during the Italian tour, speaks of his tendency to *espieglerie*, and to the treatment of men and things in a droll and consequently often pleasant fashion, and King Leopold, writing to the queen, says: "Albert is a very agreeable companion. His manners are so gentle and harmonious, that one likes to have him near one's self. I always found him so when I had him with me, and I think his travels have still further improved him. He is full of talent and fun, and draws cleverly."

Even while this was being written from Brussels, however, the youthful queen had discovered the fascinating character of her future

[1] *Early Years of the Prince Consort.*

husband. If the meeting of these two young people was not the occasion of "love at first sight," it was at least the opportunity for a revival of that early regard with the intensity of a maturer and more significant affection. On the second day after the arrival of the princes the uncertainty which had attended the visit was nearly dissipated, and on the 14th of October the queen had informed Lord Melbourne of her intention. He showed the greatest satisfaction at the announcement, adding the expression of his conviction that it would not only make her position more comfortable, but would be well received by the country.

The short story of this royal courtship, as far as we can read it in the account which the queen herself has endorsed, is very pure and sweet. There is a charming simplicity in the record, which carries us far away from the mere external trappings and ceremonious observances of a court, and yet is truly regal in its evident fidelity and confidence. What can be more charmingly ingenuous, for instance, than the letter sent by the queen to Baron Stockmar, to whom, as she had so recently expressed her resolution not to marry for some time, she wrote with a naïve embarrassment:—

"WINDSOR CASTLE, *15th October*, 1839.

"I do feel so guilty, I know not how to begin my letter; but I think the news that it will contain will be sufficient to insure your forgiveness. Albert has completely won my heart, and all was settled between us this morning. . . . I feel certain he will make me very happy. I wish I could say I felt as certain of my making him happy, but I shall do my best. Uncle Leopold must tell you all about the details, which I have not time to do. . . . Albert is very much attached to you."

On the following day the prince writes to the same old and tried friend, what he knew would be "the most welcome news possible." "Victoria," he says, "is so good and kind to me that I am often puzzled to believe that I should be the object of so much affection. I know the interest you take in my happiness, and therefore pour out my heart to you. . . . More or more seriously I cannot write: I am at this moment too much bewildered to do so.

"Das Auge sicht den Himmel offen,
Es schwelgt das Herz in Seligkeit."[1]

[1] Heaven opens on the ravish'd eye,
The heart is all entranced in bliss.
Schiller's *Song of the Bell*.

The records of the happy married life of the queen are interspersed with letters full of similar expressions of mutual affection. In the two books in which her majesty, with the simple, true womanliness that was always her characteristic, has taken her subjects into an almost sacred confidence,[1] we are shown how that early love remained full of lustre, undimmed by passing years and pressing cares of state. In the more recent *Life of the Prince Consort*, compiled and written by Mr. Theodore Martin, with the direct sanction and endorsement of the queen herself, who has added here and there a note, brief but full of tender suggestion, we have a yet fuller account not only of the domestic life of the royal family, but of the early hostilities and misapprehensions which the prince experienced, but so completely overcame by his rare sagacity, his modest patient temper, and admirable self-restraint. We see too how those very qualities by which he won the queen enabled him to win the people too, so that when he died queen and people alike were widowed, and were united in mourning their great bereavement.

It is not only those who know with what acute sensitiveness Prince Albert regarded the misunderstanding of his character, which caused people at first to regard him with caution, that the volumes to which we have referred will come as a pleasant confirmation of the opinion they learned to form of his high honour and sincerity of purpose. In the same way those who, knowing him but at a distance, detected what seemed like coldness and even hauteur in his demeanour, will in the letters and narratives find another proof that this was the external habit adopted as a precaution against a familiarity, which, if too general, would have been misconstrued and probably condemned. It may also have been the natural reticence of a man who, himself living a simple and yet a high life, was compelled, and indeed delighted to mingle with earnest workers of every grade, who yet may not have had his aims and who could scarcely estimate the difficulties of his position.

There was no lack of real sweetness, nor of a certain lowliness of heart in his character, and he never shrank from anything that he conceived to be a public duty demanded by his station, though he frequently had to undergo considerable suffering from illness, and many heart-burnings and disappointments in consequence of the mistaken estimate which some people persisted in making of his intentions. Perhaps of all the statesmen of his early time the Duke of Wellington and Sir Robert

[1] *Our Life in the Highlands. Early Years of the Prince Consort.*

feel understood and appreciated him best; but his patient consistency, and his evident desire to use his great abilities in that sphere of social material improvement which enabled him to do so much for the advancement of the everyday life of the people, and his constant modesty and temper, attracted all the really capable and appreciative men with whom he worked.

The tremendous exertions which he underwent in order to overcome the difficulties, and to insure the success of the Great Exhibition of 1851, showed of how much he was capable, both in actual organization and in admirable self-control, and the modest determination with which he refused his assent to any of the surplus funds being devoted to show him public honour was but one among many proofs of his unselfish desire to find a reward in the work that lay before him. Few men could have done that work so well, for it involved many hours of close study in his writing-room, many conferences and committees, many public meetings and public speeches, and much personal inspection and direction. It is to be feared that he too often permitted himself to undertake duties beyond the actual strength of his constitution, but he fulfilled them so cheerfully, and seemed to be capable of such recuperation during the short happy holidays that he and the queen passed at Osborne or in the Highlands, that he could throw off the apparent pressure of fatigue and excitement sooner than many men of even a more mercurial temperament.

He left the world and the country the better for the life which passed out of this sphere while it was still in the midst of activity and usefulness; but he had won a noble victory over the hearts of some of the most prejudiced of mankind, and England, almost startled into sudden pain by his illness, bowed in sorrow at the intelligence of his death, not only because he was the husband of England's queen, but because he was possessed of qualities with which the nation of his adoption might well desire to claim kin. Well might the people find in the words of the poet-laureate the outcry which came from so many hearts:—

> "We know him now : all narrow jealousies
> Are silent; and we see him as he moved,
> How modest, kindly, all-accomplish'd, wise;
> With what sublime repression of himself,
> And in what limits, and how tenderly ;
> Not swaying to this faction or to that ;

> Not making his high place the lawless perch
> Of wing'd ambitions, nor a vantage-ground
> For pleasure; but through all this tract of years
> Wearing the white flower of a blameless life,
> Before a thousand peering littlenesses,
> In that fierce light which beats upon a throne,
> And blackens every blot: for where is he
> Who dares foreshadow for an only son
> A lovelier life, a more unstain'd than his?
> Or how should England, dreaming of *his* sons,
> Hope more for these than some inheritance
> Of such a life, a heart, a mind as thine,
> Thou noble father of her kings to be,
> Laborious for her people and her poor—
> Voice in the rich dawn of an ampler day—
> Far-sighted summoner of war and waste
> To fruitful strifes and rivalries of peace—
> Sweet nature gilded by the gracious gleam
> Of letters, dear to science, dear to art,
> Dear to thy land and ours, a Prince indeed,
> Beyond all titles, and a household name
> Hereafter, thro' all times, Albert the Good!"

SUNDAY IN THE BACKWOODS.

Perhaps there is no more striking characteristic in the history of the English people than that spirit of enterprise which has made them almost universal colonists. It is of course to be observed, that all nations which have become remarkable for maritime commerce, have extended their communities in distant lands, and have either mingled with the original inhabitants or have formed distinct societies, sustaining amicable relations or destined eventually to come into conflict with the aborigines or their descendants. The Dutch, the Portuguese, the Spaniards, and some of the people of Northern Europe, have been successful colonists from early times; but among the English people there seems to survive the Anglo-Saxon talent for supplementing colonization or even successful invasion by a political and social organization which, being planted on the ground of free and elastic institutions, takes firm root and yet grows with great rapidity. It is perhaps owing to the combination of the constructive and the commercial elements in the English character that in every latitude and under all kinds of external conditions our colonies either assume a rapid development, or after a determined subjugation of the difficulties that first present themselves grow into healthy and flourishing communities with a singular adaptation to the climate and circumstances of the country in which they are established, but at the same time with a remarkable and sturdy retention of many English customs, observances, and modes of living. With a strength of constitution and a freedom of action which leaves great scope for varied conditions of existence, the Englishman combines an intense individuality and a certain half-concealed national pride, which distinguishes him all over the world. His ready adaptability stands him in better stead than that talent for acquiring foreign languages for which many European citizens are distinguished; while his distinctive nationality, partly the result of the geographical position of his country,—and even some of his prejudices, serve to maintain a certain dominance of character which peculiarly belongs to him. It may also be said that the copiousness of our language is itself an element in our success as colonists, and there is good reason to believe that English will be the universal tongue, if ever mankind should adopt one, since the English-speaking colonies represent, if we include the great American continent, not only a vast extent of territory in every quarter of the globe, but the communities which are growing in wealth, strength, and enterprise.

The rapid growth of our colonies in Australasia, and the development of what was once only a convict station to a prosperous community which bids fair to become an important and influential province, has been one of the wonders of recent times. The names of New South Wales or Van Diemen's Land have now lost their old significance, and it is to our interest as well as to that of the colonists themselves to forget it in the wider meaning of their grand commercial and colonial relations. Meanwhile, New Zealand, Queensland, Tasmania, Victoria, Southern Australia, with Adelaide, its great mercantile capital, and the Swan River Settlement, now known as Western Australia, all take their contingent of emigrants. The emigration of British subjects to Australia and New Zealand was 38,828 in 1862, and in the following year had increased to 50,157. In 1871 the figures had fallen to 11,695, but in 1872 they rose again to 15,248, in 1873 to 25,137, while in 1874 they showed the large number of 52,581, since which they have again declined to 34,750 in 1875, and 32,196 in 1876; British emigration to the United States of America having also declined from 166,730 in 1873 to 54,554 in 1876; while the numbers represented by the British colonies of North America had declined from 29,045 in 1873, to 20,728 in 1874, 12,306 in 1875, and 9335 in 1876, the foreign emigration to these British possessions representing about one-fourth more than these numbers.

Ontario and Quebec, the two older colonies of British North America, are still receiving large reinforcements from this country, though the name Canada now includes "The Dominion," which in 1867 was made by act of parliament to comprise Nova Scotia and New Brunswick also, while provision was made to admit other provinces as occasion might arise. The Dominion of Canada now means Upper and Lower Canada, New Brunswick, Nova Scotia, Prince Edward Island, British Columbia, Manitoba, and in fact the whole of British North America except Newfoundland. It is to Upper Canada or Ontario and to British Columbia, formerly a part of the Hudson's Bay territory, that the agricultural and actual colonizing emigration is directed. The population of the latter province is about 50,000, including a large number of Chinese, and it rose into importance after the discovery of gold in its rivers in 1858, when the immigration of diggers from California made it necessary for the British government to transform the territory into a regular colony. With plenty of coal and magnificent timber the country is also extremely fertile, and during the last five years has been considerably devoted to agriculture and to the raising of cereals and farm produce. Perhaps the white population does not exceed 15,000, so that there is still "room and verge enough."

The old colony of Ontario or Upper Canada continues to sustain its reputation, though there also the vast trade in timber is yielding somewhat to the claims of agriculture. In the "backwoods" vast clearings have been made since the period in which the picture reproduced in these pages was intended to represent that healthy individuality of Scottish life which found expression even in the primeval forest, where an emigrant family rested on the Sabbath from the labour that sought to make a happy homestead in the midst of that great wilderness of mighty trees by means of saw and hatchet wielded by strong arms.

Even in this free, busy, and primitive life, however, the griefs and cares that belong to humanity cannot be escaped, and there is a certain tender pathos in the aspect of the invalid girl who is so interesting a figure in Mr. Faed's charming picture, which is itself intended to represent a real scene or rather a family episode referred to in the following extract from a letter from Canada. "We have no church here, but our log home, or the wide forest, and a grand kirk the forest makes, not even the auld cathedral has such pillars, space, nor so high a roof; so we e'en take turns about on Sunday in reading the Bible. We are all well except Jeannie, and as happy as can be, considering the country and ties we have left. Poor Jeannie is sadly changed, her only song now is, 'Why left I my hame?' But for her illness our lot ought not to be an unhappy one."

It is in Quebec district, however, that the backwood settler is said to be seen to the best advantage. "If approached from the side of a forest," says Mr. Rowan, a writer of considerable authority on the subject, "the first sign of civilization is the sound of the cow-bells, which are strapped to the necks of the cattle to enable their owners to find them. A good-toned bell on a still day can be heard two or three miles off. The roads leading out of these back-settlements are of the very roughest description in the summer, but in the winter, thanks to the snow, are level and excellent. Of course as the settlement improves, the roads improve, and in a few years the back-settler's home of to-day is the centre of the settlement, accessible by good roads and possessing every advantage.

"For the first seven or eight years the back-settler leads a hard life. Having chosen his land and purchased it (one-fifth of the purchase-money being paid down and the remainder in four annual instalments) he proceeds to build himself a log-house, about 18 feet by 20 feet, which he roofs with split pine or cedar ('shingles'). Externally these log-huts are of the roughest description, no tool being laid upon them but the axe. Internally, however, if the good woman is tidy, they are comfortable enough. The back-settler, though content with a log-hut himself, puts up a more pretentious building for his hay and his cattle. His barn is generally built of boards hauled from the nearest saw-mill, and roofed either with shingles made with own hands or with spruce-bark. These buildings are situated in the centre of an open space in the forest, from which it is fenced off by the half-burned poles

arranged in what is generally called a 'ripgut' fence. The crops—potatoes, oats, and buckwheat—grow in patches amongst the black charred stumps, and grow so well too as almost to hide the latter, though they are two feet in height. Outside the fence the back-settler's stock remain about the neighbouring forest, where (says Mr. Rowan) I am afraid most of his leisure time is taken up in hunting for them. But indeed his leisure moments must be few, for a back-settler has to turn his hand to everything. He must be his own carpenter, his own blacksmith. There is no division of labour in the backwoods. The man and woman of the house do everything. The knowing old settler never breaks his back in tearing a green stump out by the roots. His *modus operandi* is somewhat as follows: In winter, when he has the time to spare, he chops a few acres of forest, hauling off the soft wood for logs, fence-rails, &c., and the hard wood for firing. The wastewood and branches he makes into piles, and burns when dry in the spring. In the space thus cleared and burned he plants potatoes with the hoe here and there in little hills among the stumps. In the following year he sows grain seed, and lays it down as pasture. After seven years the hard-wood stumps are rotten, and come out easily. The pine, owing to its resinous nature, does not rot so quickly, and gives a little more trouble. The land is now ready for the plough, and in the eighth year he takes a crop of wheat off it, and brings it into regular rotation. Say four acres of forest are chopped every year, he will thus have (after the seventh year) ten acres of new land coming in each season, viz.: five of burned land for potatoes, and five to stump and plough for wheat. The virgin soil needs no manure, and yields magnificent crops. When the settler has new land coming in each year he from time to time lays down portions of his longest cleared land in permanent pasture."

His life is not all roses; and, indeed, the roses are something he lives to enjoy in the future. The venomous flies and the mosquitoes, next to the "woful lack of cash," are his greatest trouble. But even then he has his consolation, for the greater his clearing becomes the less do these pests annoy him; they disappear with the forest. In the high lands they are not so bad, but in the swampy ground they are all but intolerable. In the valley of the Metapedia families have been known to be routed out of the country by the black flies. The cattle also are not exempt. The caribou fly, " whose bite is only a shade less severe than that of a dog," greatly annoys them, until, to obtain relief, they imitate the moose by plunging into the lakes and rivers, and there remaining during the hot portion of the June and July days.

But the backwoods have their compensating advantage. In the winter the settler is sheltered from the blasts, and he has always fuel at his hand to warm himself to his heart's content. His life is one of toil, but it is one of hope also. Every day he devotes to labour brings him a day nearer to his goal of independence. "Every hour's work he spends on his clearing makes him a richer man; every acre he ploughs, every stump even he takes out, makes his farm more valuable. All his work bears fruit, and at the end of ten or fifteen years it is wonderful to see what a transformation the industrious back-settler has made in the hole he has hewn out of the primeval forest." The rude log-hut in time gives place to a more elegant and commodious mansion. "Nothing is more common than to see on the farm of a successful settler a handsome house, and a little way off the rude log-cabin which in 'old times' gave him and his family shelter; nothing is more common than to hear the substantial farmer in Canada or the United States talking almost regretfully of the happy days he spent in the old cabin when he was poor in gold but rich in hopes and in all that makes life tolerable."[1]

Land in Lower Canada could recently be bought at prices varying from half a crown to fifteen shillings an acre, payable in instalments, the first to be paid on the day of purchase. Of course the lower price is practically giving the land away, but the qualities of soil vary considerably. The valley of the Saguenay and the valleys of the Matawan, Matepediac, and Ottawa are also regarded as good agricultural settlements. The best land is often far from the old settlements, where of course the good land has been taken up; but in these times roads and railways are rapidly made, and the settler who a few years ago was in the woods, finds himself near to a rising town and on the line of a railway which skirts his farm. In the province of Quebec the law granting "homestead land" is still in force. By this law a certain portion of a settler's property is exempted from seizure for debt for ten years after he settles on the land: a great advantage to the enterprising man, who is thus protected without his credit being

[1] *The Countries of the World;* by Dr. Robert Brown.

destroyed, but a disadvantage to the first creditors of a dishonest speculator, who in England would be liable to distraint and in Scotland to the law of hypothec.

In Quebec, though the greater number of the people are French, both the English and French languages are spoken, but the same patriotic loyalty to "the Dominion" animates all alike. A million of French people, or people of Gallic descent, live contentedly under British rule; but they are the French of the *ancien régime*, of the old monarchy, know nothing of republics, and speak a dialect which their fathers spoke in the days of Louis Quatorze. Without ever having seen or expecting to see France, for which they have only a sentimental feeling, they retain their national traits. They are protected in their religion by the government. They have their own schools and their own priests, and live under a primitive sacerdotal rule which appears strangely out of place in the New World. In 1759, when they passed under British rule, the French numbered 65,000; at present, by the census of 1871, their descendants are 1,082,940, and it was believed that there would be considerable additions from Alsace and Lorraine after they were annexed by Germany.

In his very interesting account of the French people of Quebec under British rule Dr. Robert Brown says it must be acknowledged that they are extremely ignorant, and that the priests exercise an iron rule in controlling education and in levying the tithes and other church dues from its adherents. Quebec accordingly preserves the last remnant of a state church in America, and some of its sees and conventual institutions are extremely wealthy. The French in Canada also live under their old laws, except in those cases in which they have preferred to substitute the English criminal law and trial by jury for the old arbitrary rule of "intendants," and such like representations of the despotic French monarchy which existed prior to the revolution of 1792. In Quebec are found the greatest number of owners and occupiers of land under ten acres, and as the French custom of inheritance obtains there a continual subdivision is going on among members of the same family. One effect of this is to be seen in the district below Quebec and between that place and Montreal, especially on the south side of the St. Lawrence, where the number of small homesteads give almost the appearance of a village street. In the course of a few generations a large farm becomes divided into a number of homesteads, each scarcely capable of supporting the family residing upon it, and too small to admit of further severance. Up to 1854 the seignorial tenures of old France prevailed, and their influence is still so far felt that in Quebec holders of more than 200 acres are also more common than in the other provinces.

THE GRAND DURBAR AT CAWNPORE,

NOVEMBER 3, 1859.

The more recent public events which have distinguished the present period scarcely yet belong to the domain of history, and few of them have been made the subjects of historical pictures. The vast and rapid progress made by this country during the last quarter of a century baffles the effort to represent either pictorially or by brief description the successive stages of the national advance, nor has a period so crowded with important achievements found many interpreters capable of translating even its more prominent occurrences into the language of art.

One of the foremost of these, the visit of the heir to the throne to India, gave occasion for so many vivid and picturesque descriptions in the public journals that it may some day form the subject of more than one historical painting, especially as the journey made by the prince to the various dependencies had some effect in consolidating the loyalty of representative native rulers and their feudal subjects. That visit may be said to have been an endorsement of the conciliatory measures which were taken after the end of the Indian mutiny in order to confirm the allegiance of native princes and to attest the determination of the English government to rule in accordance with a clement imperial policy.

The relief of Lucknow had followed the taking of Delhi, and the great remaining difficulty was the pacification and territorial settlement of the kingdom of Oude, which was placed under the control of a chief commissioner. The harsh measures by which confiscation of the property of native land-owners was contemplated aroused considerable opposition not only on the part of the East India Company, but in parliament, and it was not till the general scheme of the future government of India was accepted that the question could be finally decided. On the 8th of July, 1858, the India Bill passed the House of Commons, on the 23d it passed the House of Lords, and on the 2d of August, the last day of the session, it received the assent of the crown. By its provisions the East India Company was dissolved, and to quote the words of the bill, "all the powers in relation to government vested in or exercised by the said Company in trust for her majesty, shall cease to be vested in or exercised by the said Company, and all territories in the possession or under the government of the said Company, and all rights vested, or which, if this act had not been passed, might have been exercised by the said Company in relation to any territories, shall become vested in her majesty and be exercised in her name; and for the purposes of this act India shall mean the territories vested in her majesty as aforesaid, and all territories which may become vested in her majesty by virtue of any such rights as aforesaid."

The mutiny was practically at an end. A strong garrison had been left in Lucknow, and the hill forts in Rohilcund to which the rebels had retired were taken and their defenders put to flight. Sir Colin Campbell had directed these movements with consummate skill, courage, and perseverance, and for his distinguished services was elevated to the peerage with the title of Lord Clyde. A general pacification was promoted by the transference of the entire government of India to the British crown, and when the royal proclamation was published by the governor-general, Lord Canning, on the 1st of November, 1858, it called forth several native addresses to the queen expressive of loyalty and attachment. The proclamation itself was well calculated at once to impress and to conciliate the native chiefs and their followers. It announced that all engagements which had been made with the native princes by the East India Company would be scrupulously maintained and fulfilled, that no extension of territorial possession was sought, and that no aggression upon it should be tolerated or encroachment upon that of others sanctioned. It held the British government bound to the natives of our Indian territories by the same obligations of duty which bound it to the other subjects of the British Empire. Upon the important subject of religion, in which the rebellion was said to have originated, the declaration said: "Firmly relying ourselves on the truth of Christianity, and acknowledging with gratitude the solace of religion, we disclaim alike the right and the desire to impose our conviction on any of our subjects. We declare it to be our royal will and pleasure that none be in any wise favoured, none molested or disquieted, by reason of their religious faith or observances, but that all shall alike enjoy the equal and impartial protection of the law; and we do strictly charge and enjoin all those who may be in authority under us, that they abstain from all interference with the religious belief or worship of any of our subjects, on pain of our highest displeasure." It was added that all of whatever race or creed were to be freely and impartially admitted to such offices in her majesty's service as they were qualified to hold. Those who inherited lands were to be protected in all rights connected therewith subject to the equitable demands of the state, and in framing and administering the law due regard was to be paid to the ancient rights, usages, and customs of India. With regard to the late rebellion the proclamation declared:—"Our clemency will be extended to all offenders, save and except those who have been or shall be convicted of having directly taken part in the murder of British subjects. With regard to such, the demands of justice forbid the exercise of mercy. To those who have willingly given an asylum to murderers, knowing them to be such, their lives alone can be guaranteed; but in apportioning the penalty due to such persons full consideration will be given to any circumstances under which they have been induced to throw off their allegiance; and large indulgence will be shown to those whose crimes may appear to have originated in too credulous acceptance of the false reports circulated by designing men. To all others in arms against the government we hereby promise unconditional pardon, amnesty, and oblivion of all offence against ourselves, our crown, and dignity, on their return to their homes and peaceful pursuits. It is our royal pleasure that these terms of grace and amnesty should be extended to all those who comply with these conditions before the 1st day of January next. When, by the blessing of Providence, internal tranquillity shall be restored, it is our earnest desire to stimulate the peaceful industry of India, to promote works of public utility and

improvement, and to administer its government for the benefit of all our subjects therein. In their prosperity will be our strength, in their contentment our security, and in their gratitude our best reward. And may the God of all power grant to us, and to those in authority under us, strength to carry out these our wishes for the good of our people!"[1]

The proclamation promised an amnesty to all those who returned to peaceful pursuits and to their homes before the 1st of January, 1859, but much had to be accomplished for the final pacification of Oude, where the Begum issued a counter proclamation. The rebels had made this province their place of shelter and rallying point, and such decisive measures had to be adopted as could only be justified by the necessity of the case and the dangerous attitude of the enemy. Fort after fort was taken, however, and that of Shunkerpoor, for the reduction of which the whole British force in the district had been concentrated, was at last surrendered by Bainee Madhoo, an insurgent chief, who escaped probably to the hills of Nepaul, where only a cold reception awaited the vanquished rebels. Thither Nana Sahib was driven after a ruinous defeat, to become an outcast and a hunted fugitive, and to this quarter also his brother Bala Rao betook himself, after attempting a final stand in which his troops were beaten and dispersed almost without resistance. During this time, however, the pacification of the province was being effected by the constant submission of chiefs who went to the chief commissioner at Lucknow to tender their adhesion; and though desultory hostilities continued for some time afterwards they were all successfully checked, the contest in Oude was brought to an end, and the resistance of 150,000 armed men had been subdued with a very moderate loss to the British force, and with remarkable forbearance towards the misguided rebels.

On the 12th of October, 1859, the governor-general commenced a tour through the provinces, and his journey may be said to have represented a royal progress, marked at the principal stations by the assembling of grand durbars or levees, to which the loyal chiefs were invited, and where they were received with due magnificence, that they might be presented with robes of honour, collars, chains, and various ornaments in recognition of their allegiance during the mutiny.

The most imposing of these ceremonies was the Grand Durbar which was held at Cawnpore on the 3d of November, 1859, at two

[1] *History of India. Comprehensive History of England.*

o'clock in the day, in a great tent lined with yellow. In the centre of the farther side of this tent was Lord Canning's chair, on his right was all the rajahs, on his left the chair of the commander-in-chief, and beyond that, the places reserved for Sir Richmond Shakespear, Generals Birch and Mansfield, Colonel Beecher, and Colonel Stuart. Behind them the governor-general and chief's staff, and then a number of civilians, beyond whom were about 200 military officers. By the appointed time all were in their seats, and the sight was a gorgeous one, because of the great variety of costumes and the brilliancy of colour. The representative rajah in point of magnificence was he of Rewah, who occupied a chair on the right hand of the viceroy. He was described at the time as a big burly man of tall stature, with a heavy grossly sensual face, and yellow complexion. His hands, fat and shapeless, were covered with dazzling rings. He wore a light yellow tunic with a black and white scarf that looked at a distance like a boa-constrictor's skin. On his head was a handsome towering cap composed entirely of gold and diamonds, which evidently made an inclination of the head difficult. On his right sat Mr. Cecil Beadon, the home and foreign secretary, and next him the Benares rajah, quietly dressed and with a white shawl turban. Next him again was the rajah of Chikaree, an elderly handsome man dressed in red; and besides there were above a hundred other chiefs of various degrees, not two of whom were similarly attired, so that the contrasts of colour were remarkable, and often very striking. A passage-tent kept by the grenadier company of the 35th Regiment as a guard of honour led to the durbar tent, and soon after two o'clock the military orders, concluding with "Present arms!" announced the arrival of the viceroy, whose presence was saluted by the firing of a round of guns. He entered the durbar tent preceded by his chief secretaries of state and aides-de-camp, the assembly rising on his entrance, and remaining standing till he reached the chair of state and sat down.

Then came the presentations of the rajahs, Mr. Beadon, the home and foreign secretary, introducing the more important chiefs, and another officer the less distinguished ones. Each rajah made his most graceful obeisance, an act accompanied in every case with a nuzzur (or present), which was also in each case, after being touched by the vice-regal hand, taken from the officer by the people of the Tosha Khana department.

Then came the presentation of khelats. The principal rajahs had chains fastened on their necks, but only to one, the Rewah rajah, was this done by Lord Canning personally. To give him his chain his lordship rose and passed it round his neck. The others had their collars of honour put on by the secretaries, Lord Canning merely touching each chain when presented to him for that purpose.

The Rewah rajah, the Benares rajah, and the Chikaree rajah were each addressed by Lord Canning in English on their khelats being given them; but to the Chikaree rajah a great honour was paid, for, after saying a few words to him, Lord Canning, turning to the commander-in-chief, who on being addressed immediately stood up, the whole of the English officers present standing also, said, "Lord Clyde, I wish to bring to your notice the conduct of this brave man, who showed marked devotion to the British cause by acting on the offensive against the rebels of his own accord, and when besieged in a fort refused to give up a British officer, offering his own son as a hostage instead; and I trust." said Lord Canning. "that every officer of the queen now present will remember this, and should they ever come in contact with this rajah, act accordingly."

This was the crowning ceremony of the Great Durbar at Cawnpore, which may itself be regarded as the special demonstration of the British government to imply that by the pacification of the province where some of the foulest deeds of the mutiny had been committed, and where the rebellion made its last ineffectual stand, the authority of the queen had been established, and the relation between India and Great Britain had been permanently restored.

THE END.

www.ingramcontent.com/pod-product-compliance
Lightning Source LLC
Chambersburg PA
CBHW031735230426
43669CB00007B/352